Engagement and the Language of the Subject
in the Poetry of Aimé Césaire

University of Florida Monographs
Humanities Number 59

Engagement and the Language of the Subject
in the Poetry of Aimé Césaire

Ronnie Leah Scharfman

University Presses of Florida

UNIVERSITY OF FLORIDA PRESS
Gainesville

Library of Congress Cataloging-in-Publication Data

Scharfman, Ronnie Leah.
  Engagement and the language of the subject in
the poetry of Aimé Césaire.

  (University of Florida monographs. Humanities;
no. 59)
  Bibliography: p.
  Includes index.
  1. Césaire, Aimé—Criticism and interpretation.
2. Politics in literature.   3. Blacks in literature.
4. Race awareness in literature.   5. Colonies in
literature.   I. Title.   II. Series.
PQ3949.C44Z864   1987   841   86–16162
ISBN 0–8130–0822–0

UNIVERSITY PRESSES OF FLORIDA is the central agency for scholarly publishing of the
State of Florida's university system, producing books selected for publication by the faculty
editorial committees of Florida's nine public universities: Florida A&M University (Tallahassee),
Florida Atlantic University (Boca Raton), Florida International University (Miami), Florida
State University (Tallahassee), University of Central Florida (Orlando), University of Florida
(Gainesville), University of North Florida (Jacksonville), University of South Florida (Tampa),
University of West Florida (Pensacola).

ORDERS for books published by all member presses should be addressed to University Presses
of Florida, 15 NW 15th Street, Gainesville, FL 32603.

Printed in the U.S.A. on acid-free paper ∞

Acknowledgments

THIS BOOK could not have been written without the inspiration of Professor Antoine Raybaud of the Universités de Genève and d'Aix- en-Provence, mentor, teacher and friend, who first taught me how to read Césaire. My gratitude toward my professors at Yale, especially Shoshana Felman and the late Paul de Man, under whose guidance this manuscript first took form, is manifest in the nature of its inquiry. I would also like to thank Professor Léon-François Hoffmann of Princeton for his careful reading and valuable suggestions; Dr. G. Rose for his encouragement; and the jury of the Institut Français de Washington, which awarded this manuscript a Gilbert Chinard Literary Prize in 1982. Finally, the patience and support of my husband, who listened, counselled, read, and edited, are really what allowed this project to come to fruition. Thanks go also to the Graduate School of the University of Florida for making this publication possible.

Quotations are used by permission of the following publishers.

Editions du Seuil
Aimé Césaire, *Cadastre*. Translated by Emile Snyder and Sanford Upson. Bilingual edition. Paris, 1961.
Aimé Césaire, *Ferrements*. Paris, 1960.
Frantz Fanon, *Peau noire, masques blancs*. 2d edition. Paris, 1975.

Présence Africaine
Aimé Césaire, *Cahier d'un retour au pays natal*. Translated by Emile Snyder. Bilingual edition. Preface by André Breton. 3d edition. Paris, 1971.
Aimé Césaire, "Poésie et connaissance." From *Aimé Césaire, l'homme et l'œuvre* by Lilyan Kesteloot and Barthélemy Kotchy. Paris, 1973.

Editions Gallimard
Aimé Césaire, *Les Armes miraculeuses*. 2d edition. Paris, 1970.
Jean-Paul Sartre, "Orphée noir." Introduction to *Anthologie de la nouvelle poésie nègre et malgache de langue française,* ed. Léopold Sédar Senghor. 2d ed. Paris: Presses Universitaires de France, 1969.

Contents

For
Joseph, Ethan and Zachary

Introduction

WITH THE recent publication of two major volumes in this country, the work of the Martinican poet Aimé Césaire can finally reach the English-speaking reader in a meaningful way. It is a fitting and moving tribute to this great poet, playwright, essayist, and political activist that his *Collected Poetry,* magnificently translated by Clayton Eshleman and Annette Smith, gloriously illustrated with works by Wifredo Lam, should appear in such a beautiful bilingual edition in 1983, the year of Césaire's seventieth birthday. The translation is a stunning accomplishment, given the difficulties of the Césairian text. In their introduction the translators themselves point to "the schizophrenic exercise one goes through when translating Césaire," noting also that "the problems raised by the syntax, however, are far from equaling the lexicological ones." [1]

Two years earlier, the first significant introduction to Césaire's life and work was published in English. A. James Arnold's *Modernism and Negritude: The Poetry and Poetics of Aimé Césaire* is a comprehensive and thoroughly researched study, which places both Césaire and his work in their social, political, historical, and literary contexts. These two books can be read felicitously as companion pieces, each illuminating the other. Their publication testifies to the growing recognition that Césaire's œuvre is receiving in the Anglophone world, and their appearance should be hailed.

Yet even in the Francophone world, the difficulty of Césaire's corpus has baffled critics outside of those Third World countries where his appeal as a spokesman for cultural decolonization was immediate. Despite André Breton's "discovery" of the *Cahier* in 1941, in which he declared that "ce poème n'était rien moins que le plus grand monument lyrique de ce temps," and the critical authority which Jean-Paul Sartre's "Orphée noir" essay lent to Césaire's poetic project, Michel Leiris felt he needed to entitle an article dated 1965, "Qui est Aimé Césaire?" [2] It is not surprising that a powerful œuvre such as Césaire's has often been criticized as "hermetic" and "exotic," on the one hand, and politically subversive or limited by the ideology of negritude, on the other. But the absence of a problematic that would simultaneously ar-

1. *The Collected Poetry,* pp. 25–26.
2. André Breton, "Un Grand Poète noir," p. 17; Jean-Paul Sartre, "Orphée noir," pp. ix–xliv; Michel Leiris, "Qui est Aimé Césaire?" pp. 7–16.

1

ticulate the difficulties of Césaire's poetic discourse and its political *engagement* leaves a gap in the field of Césaire criticism which this book seeks to reduce.

In *Modernism and Negritude,* Arnold acknowledges this problem, calling it a "paradox of the negritude movement that it simultaneously cultivated a rhetoric of protest and an intensely subjective poetics: the one discursive and polemical, turned towards the world; the other, lyrical and looking inward to a personal renewal, turned toward a form of spiritual salvation or revelation."[3] It is precisely this paradox and its textual functioning that are explored in this study, contributing in a new way to Césaire criticism.

In order to approach Césaire's poetry, the question of the status of the subject must be confronted. For the subject that speaks in the poetic texts recognizes itself as alienated and subverted, and the poetry that it produces is subversive. *Engagement and the Language of the Subject* focuses on the subject, operating through detailed readings of several of the poems in their entirety. But it is not meant to illustrate a preconceived thesis. The purpose is rather to expose the way texts pose certain questions, in the hope of defining a problematic. Such an approach seeks to dilate literary problems rather than resolve them. In this sense, this essay differs from two fine, previous studies of Césaire's poetry which have paved the way for it.

In *Proposition poétique: Une lecture de l'œuvre d'Aimé Césaire,* Bernadette Cailler has organized her discussion around poetic categories that Césaire outlines at the end of his important article "Poésie et connaissance" and which he calls "propositions." The value of this kind of "Césaire par lui-même" is great, and it has been executed with great insight and sensitivity. A procedure that utilizes such a grid is, however, problematic. First, it cannot account for the way in which any specific text functions. Second, applying an author's critical prose discourse to a properly poetic one demands a problematization of the relationship between the two, which Cailler does not outline clearly.

Keith Walker uses a thematic method inspired by the works of Gaston Bachelard in his attempt to reveal *La Cohésion poétique de l'œuvre césairienne.* By analyzing the poet's repeated use of cosmic elements, colors, flora, beasts, and other fauna, Walker exposes a unified affective network in which anguish and simplicity, violence and peace, humanity and negritude all have a place. Walker gives us a reassuring reading of Césaire which places him within the humanist tradition. Yet Césaire claims to be the poetic heir of Lautréamont, Mallarmé, and Rimbaud, among others—dark poets whose texts deconstruct the kind of luminous cohesiveness Walker's arguments would

3. Arnold, *Modernism and Negritude,* pp. 58–59.

construct. Césaire's text is very demanding of its readers, pushing them beyond habitual structures of categorization. As early as 1941, Breton had already characterized Césaire's obscurity: "La poésie digne de ce nom s'évalue au degré d'abstention, de *refus* qu'elle suppose et ce côté négateur de sa nature exige d'être tenu pour constitutif. . . . Césaire est à cet égard des plus *difficiles* et cela non seulement parce qu'il est la probité même mais encore dans la mesure où son savoir est plus étendu, où il est à la fois des mieux et des plus largement informés." [4] If the refusal is poetic, it is also political, and the problematic nature of the articulation of both is what will be of concern to us here.

Because the colonial situation from which Césaire's text emanates is in its essence a dramatic one, that is, polarized and conflictual, many Césairian critics have chosen to examine his theater, reading it as an objective representation of the colonial structures of oppression and the various possible reactions to them.[5] Although the colonial referent cannot be ignored in any discussion of Césaire's œuvre, an approach that concentrates on the plays does not confront the complex problems of the politically committed writing subject, nor does it attempt to raise the textual question of Césaire's passage from poet to playwright. All critics comply in speaking of Césaire's *engagement,* but the fundamental gap that exists between the capacity of the subject to constitute itself in discourse and some phenomenological concept of a self that would be designated as *engagé* has nowhere been adequately addressed.

Ironically, Césaire's text speaks to this gap on every page. Like the text of Rimbaud, which hovers over it as illumination and condemnation, the poetry of Césaire tells us that "je est un autre." The forms in which this otherness is clothed are staggering in their complexity, heightened further by the colonial context. Perhaps critics have ignored the crisis of the subject in this text for fear that its deconstruction might invalidate its political message. But this is to ignore the scrupulous integrity of Césaire's poetry, which is permeated not only with a sense of the arbitrariness of language but also with doubts as to the very possibility of mediating between the individual and the collective. Perhaps, after all, *engagement* is only a poetic figure, a synecdoche which permits the subject the illusion of passage from solitude to solidarity for the brief moment that is a poem. What does a poem achieve? Do these texts bear the mark of some failure? Are we dealing with a corpus that, like Rimbaud's, pushes to a limit beyond which there can be only poetic silence, or is the Cé-

---

4. Breton, "Un Grand Poète noir," p. 19.

5. See, for example, Rodney E. Harris, *L'Humanisme dans le théâtre d'Aimé Césaire,* and Georges Ngal, "Le Théâtre d'Aimé Césaire: Une dramaturgie de la décolonisation."

sairian subject's modulation from poetry to the theater a new formulation, a new textualization of the same problems that, without the poetry, could never have evolved? These, it seems to us, are some of the questions that the text demands that we ask.

As for negritude, it is perceived as difference, from either a white or a black perspective. When we recognize that Césaire's text emanates from the violent conflict of the colonial context, then it becomes possible to read this poetry as an effort at reevaluating black difference as positive, as an aggression-transgression against the hierarchical values implicit in the binary oppositions white/black, master/slave, colonizer/colonized, capitalist/exploited, Europe/ The Antilles (or Africa), technology/nature, and so forth. Arnold aptly describes this dynamic as "The dialectics of blackness" and fully analyzes its mechanism in his discussion of the *Cahier* in the chapter entitled "The Epic of Negritude." In our readings of the *Cahier,* our critical voices often merge.[6] The situation of the black man is most certainly articulated in the poetry in conflictual terms. But we are concerned with lyric poetry as a particular discourse of the subject, which requires that we focus our critical attentions on the ways in which that subject is dramatized textually.

This essay falls into two parts. The first chapter gives a brief account of "critical models of *engagement.*" The works discussed there are to a certain extent theoretical, drawing on philosophy, sociology, political science, economics, and psychology. *Engagement* describes a reactional mode to one form of alienated consciousness, and poetry another, so that the structures that these models enable us to lay bare, be they the dialectics of otherness and the ensuing relations of power or the modes of mediating from the particular to the general, have extensive literary applications that have informed our readings. Negritude and *engagement* can be read thematically; the subject's relationship to them can be read structurally, rhetorically, and psychoanalytically.

The subsequent chapters treat the various ways in which a specific text articulates these problems and attempts to resolve them. What a poem invites us to accept on one level it often deconstructs on another. Apparent simplicity can be misleading. On the other hand, the most complex texts are often the working through of a particular solution to that poem's problems. The solutions, however, like the problems, are bound by the time/space of each poem. We read each text as an enactment of some conflict by or for the subject. The subject's self-imposed containment within the confines of poetic form has great metaphorical value. After the expansive explorations of the *Cahier,* Césaire takes up the challenge of this willed imprisonment in texts that become progressively shorter and tighter. Like Houdini, the subject experiments with

6. See Arnold, *Modernism and Negritude,* pp. 155ff.

its power to liberate itself from its own traps. The psychic function of such an exercise for a subject haunted by the memory of slavery should not be underestimated. Whether the subject can exist beyond the text, beyond that moment of potential textual liberation, is a question that any projected relationship that aspires to transcending the individual must confront. It is our aim to demonstrate the functions of such confrontation in Césaire's poetry.

1. Critical Models of *Engagement*

I<small>T IS MY</small> intention, in this chapter, to examine five essays that function as models for the problematic of *engagement* as it informs the textual readings that will follow in the rest of this study. These are Jean-Paul Sartre's "Orphée noir," Albert Memmi's *Portrait du colonisé,* Frantz Fanon's *Peau noire, masques blancs* and *Les Damnés de la terre,* and Fredric Jameson's "Imaginary and Symbolic in Lacan: Marxism, Psychoanalytic Criticism, and the Problem of the Subject." The first of these, Sartre's article, may be summarily described as an apologia for that subjective discourse that is poetry, within the framework of a revolutionary situation, the colonial one, and of a concept, negritude. The next three studies, by Memmi and Fanon, analyze those aspects of the colonial situation where the subject is inserted in a dialectical relationship of otherness to the oppressor. Finally, Jameson investigates texts that deal with the "crisis of the subject" in an effort to mediate between Marxist and psychoanalytic criticism.

Sartre's essay is important to this study in several ways. It is a major thematic discussion of the poetry of negritude, in particular Césaire's, and it is placed as the introductory text to Senghor's *Anthologie de la nouvelle poésie nègre et malgache de langue française.* As such, and Sartre himself states as much, it is meant to serve as a mediating text between black poetry and its presumed white audience. This purpose places Sartre, as a writing subject, in a politically committed situation in which he is rhetorically identified with the Césaire of the *Cahier:* "Je serais la bouche de ceux qui n'ont point de bouche." [1] This identification is a prerequisite for eliciting Sartre's inimitable combination of brilliant analysis, passionate *engagement,* and good intentions in the service of a worthy cause. His sympathy and admiration for Césaire are nowhere more evident than in the lyrical prose that Césaire's poems inspire him to write and that strains to espouse the Césairian text itself:

> Voici l'apothéose des poux de la misère noire sautant parmi les cheveux de l'eau, "îles" au fil de la lumière, craquant sous les doigts de l'épouilleuse céleste, l'aurore aux doigts de rose, cette aurore de la culture grecque et méditerranéenne, arrachée par un voleur noir aux sacrosaints poèmes homériques, et dont les ongles de la princesse en esclavage sont asservis soudain par un Toussaint Louverture à faire éclater les triomphants parasites de la mer nègre, l'au-

---

1. See chap. 2, "The Subject of the *Cahier.*"

6

rore qui soudain se rebelle et se métamorphose, verse le feu comme l'arme sauvage des blancs, lance-flamme, . . . foudroie de son feu blanc le grand Titan noir qui se relève intact, éternel, pour monter à l'assaut de l'Europe et du ciel.[2]

Sartre's overly romantic view of Césaire's poetry blinds him to certain difficulties in the text, which will be discussed. It also forces him to integrate it into his dialectical system in such a way as to have gained for this essay, ironically, the epithet of "racist" in black circles. For his extreme vision of this poetry pits it as a limited, antithetical value to the thesis of white supremacy: "En fait, la Négritude apparaît comme le temps faible d'une progression dialectique . . . la position de la Négritude comme valeur antithétique est le moment de la négativité. . . . Ainsi la Négritude est pour se détruire" (p. xli).

However, this somewhat reductive recuperation of negritude into the dialectical schema should not be allowed to blur the clarity of the rest of Sartre's argument. On the contrary, it attests indirectly to the very subversive power of this poetry of otherness which Sartre lauds at different moments in his text. We might say that in spite of his efforts, in spite of the fact that the essay proposes innumerable definitions of negritude, Sartre assimilates what is revolutionary in this poetry yet cannot, by definition, grant it its blackness.[3] He is obliged as a white man to perceive its otherness and somehow falls short of comprehending a certain aspect of its specificity.

But the otherness that Sartre defends within a Marxist framework is of primary importance here, because it concerns subjectivity and poetic discourse. The main thrust of the first part of Sartre's argument is found in the distinction drawn between the situation of the white proletariat and that of the black worker, a distinction made in terms of objective versus subjective situation and, by extension, expressed respectively in pragmatic or poetic discourse:

> Si le prolétariat blanc use rarement de la langue poétique pour parler de ses souffrances . . . ce n'est pas un hasard; . . . ce sont les circonstances actuelles de la lutte des classes qui détournent l'ouvrier de s'exprimer poétiquement. . . . Rationalisme, matérialisme, positivisme, ces grands thèmes de la

2. Sartre, "Orphée noir" (Paris: Editions Gallimard, 1969), p. xxviii. Further references to this essay appear in the text in parentheses.
3. Following are some examples of Sartre's definitions of *négritude* which punctuate "Orphée noir": "la subjectivité noire . . . un exil . . . une quête orphique . . . la négativité . . . ce poème de Césaire . . . une synthèse des aspirations révolutionnaires et du souci poétique . . . l'être-dans-le-monde-du-nègre . . . une compréhension par sympathie . . . une mémoire collective . . . un Devenir . . . dialectique . . . le contenu de poème . . . le poète lui-même . . . le triomphe du narcissisme, le suicide de Narcisse."

bataille quotidienne sont les moins propices à la création spontanée de mythes
poétiques . . . il s'agit de reconnaître dans et par l'action la situation objective
du prolétariat, qui peut se définir par les circonstances de la production ou de la
répartition des biens. . . . les travailleurs ne connaissent guère les contradictions intérieures qui fécondent l'œuvre d'art et nuisent à la praxis. . . . Tout
cela tend à l'élimination . . . du sujet. (pp. xii–xiii)

These, then, are the reasons Sartre gives for why there is no white, politically engaged poetry. The black worker, also alienated, is in a slightly different situation. Although he is similarly oppressed and victimized by capitalist
society, there is the undeniable racist element to this oppression. For Sartre,
this forces the man of color into an "authentic," subjective, awakening:

> . . . puisqu'on l'opprime dans sa race et à cause d'elle, c'est d'abord de sa
> race qu'il lui faut prendre conscience. . . . mais cette prise de conscience diffère
> en nature de celle que le marxisme tente d'éveiller chez l'ouvrier blanc. . . .
> Puisque le mépris intéressé que les blancs affichent pour les noirs . . . vise à
> toucher ceux-ci au profond du coeur, il faut que les nègres lui opposent une vue
> plus juste de la subjectivité noire. (pp. xiii–xv)

Subjectivity, then, reintervenes coextensively with negritude, in a moment
and in a movement of opposition. Poetry is founded in this relationship for
Sartre:

> Ainsi le noir qui revendique sa négritude dans un mouvement révolutionnaire se
> place d'emblée sur le terrain de la Réflexion, soit qu'il veuille retrouver en lui
> certains traits objectivement constatés dans les civilisations africaines, soit qu'il
> espère découvrir l'Essence noire dans le puits de son coeur. Ainsi reparaît la
> subjectivité, rapport de soi-même avec soi, source de toute poésie dont le tra-
> vailleur a dû se mutiler. (p. xv)

Perhaps the best validation for this aspect of Sartre's argument comes from
Césaire himself. Aside from the poetry, which is a staging and a problematiz-
ing of these considerations, there is another text of Césaire's whose rhetoric
supports Sartre's analysis, the *Lettre à Maurice Thorez*. Having been long a
member, Césaire resigned from the French Communist Party on October 24,
1956. He outlined his reasons in a letter to Thorez, then its head. Like many
intellectuals at the time, Césaire was disillusioned by the party's support of
Stalinism and of the French position in Algeria. But, more important, as the
language of the following excerpt shows, it is communism's exigence of the
dissolution of black specificity which Césaire cannot abide. This quotation
has paradigmatic value for our own problematic:

. . . le communisme . . . a achevé de nous couper de l'Afrique noire dont l'évolution se dessine désormais à contresens de la nôtre. Et pourtant cette Afrique noire, la mère de notre culture et de notre civilisation antillaise, c'est d'elle que j'attends la régénération des Antilles; pas de l'Europe qui ne peut que parfaire notre aliénation, mais de l'Afrique qui seule peut revitaliser, repersonnaliser les Antilles. . . . Je ne m'enterre pas dans un particularisme étroit. Mais je ne veux pas non plus me perdre dans un universalisme décharné. . . . Ma conception de l'universel est celle d'un universal riche de tout le particulier, riche de tous les particuliers, . . . coexistence de tous les particuliers.[4]

In response, Césaire established his own political party in Martinique, but it is also not surprising that his poetic activity was at its zenith at this time, an activity marked by the tension of a constant struggle to mediate between the particular and the universal, to forge, in effect, a black, engaged poetry.

To return to Sartre's argument, then, we have seen that he valorizes the black subject's project in poetic discourse. He then proceeds to analyze the nature of that poetic discourse in a way that links it to the modern poetic project in general. If the goals of these two poetries are divergent, their attitudes toward language and their poetic methods are similar. For the black man is also alienated culturally. Writing in French, "le noir installe en lui l'appareil-à-penser de l'ennemi" (p. xviii). This only serves to heighten "ce sentiment d'échec devant le langage considéré comme moyen d'expression directe" (p. xix). The attempt to effect disalienation, then, through language, is a kind of double bind. Although Sartre does not say it in so many words, Césaire's poetry is permeated with it, and it is a corollary to the Lacanian doctrine of the subversion of the subject by language. Sartre does affirm that modern poetic discourse is self-consciously aware of its own ambiguities: "Destructions, autodafé de langage, symbolisme magique, ambivalence des concepts, toute la poésie moderne est là, sous son aspect négatif" (p. xxiii). And Sartre inserts negritude poetry within the modern tradition, but he is so intent on emphasizing the disalienating function of black poetry that he glosses over Césaire's tragic awareness of its paradoxical nature. For Sartre, the way out of this bind is to "thematize negritude," as if that itself were not a function of language.

Nonetheless, the thematic introduction that Sartre gives Césaire's poetry in his essay is accurate and illuminating. In particular, he stresses the important role of desire in these texts, incorporating it into what he calls the subjective method of revealing negritude:

4. Césaire, *Lettre à Maurice Thorez,* quoted in Thomas Hale, ed., *Les Écrits d'Aimé Césaire,* p. 367.

Césaire . . . descendra le chemin royal de son âme . . . pour toucher . . .
l'eau noire . . . du désir et s'y laisser noyer. . . . Du désir qui fait de l'homme
un refus de tout et un amour de tout; du désir, négation radicale des lois na-
turelles et du possible, appel au miracle; du désir qui par sa folle énergie cos-
mique replonge l'homme au sein bouillonnant de la Nature par l'affirmation de
son Droit à l'insatisfaction. (pp. xxiv–xxv)

Once again, Sartre waxes poetic in speaking of Césaire in a way that both
exposes and obfuscates one of the central issues of his poetry. Sartre imagines
the poet as passively invaded by a desire that then unites him with the universe
and with his own highest aspirations. Language is curiously absent from this
scenario. And yet, as I hope to show in the detailed textual readings of succeeding chapters, it is not only in language that the subject's desire is revealed
to it, but it is also in language that the impossible gap between the subject and
its desire is articulated. The alienation of the subject in language is more fundamental than the one described by the parameters of the colonial situation,
although the structure of the latter informs the former. The purpose and scope
of Sartre's essay, as well as his own philosophical prejudice, prevent him from
examining the problematics of the functioning of Césaire's poems. He does
not, for example, question the profound pessimism and solitude of many of
the would-be engaged texts. Yet in stressing the desiring subject as the source
of Césaire's poetry, and in granting that subject the right, if not necessarily the
power, to speak in opposition to the white other, Sartre lends great validity to
Césaire's poetic project, often accused of being too hermetic:

L'originalité de Césaire est d'avoir coulé son souci étroit et puissant de nègre,
d'opprimé et de militant dans le monde de la poésie la plus destructrice, la plus
libre et la plus métaphysique, au moment où Eluard et Aragon échouaient à don-
ner un contenu politique à leurs vers. (p. xxviii)

Albert Memmi's *Portrait du colonisé* shares Sartre's dialectical view of the
relationship between the two protagonists in the colonial drama, the colonizer
and the colonized. Indeed, Sartre wrote the preface to the original 1957 edition of the *Portrait du colonisé,* and he would surely agree with Memmi's
statement that "la situation coloniale fabrique des colonialistes comme elle
fabrique des colonisés."[5] Unlike Sartre, however, Memmi gives us portraits
of colonizer and colonized from the inside, as it were. The structures he describes derive from direct experience. They are more general and less theoretical than Sartre's. But, like Césaire, Memmi speaks as one who is colo-

---

5. Albert Memmi, *Portrait du colonisé* (Paris: Petite Bibliothèque Payot, 1973),
p. 85. Further references appear in the text in parentheses.

nized and yet dangerously privileged. He was educated in France, writes in French, and, having acquired French culture, is painfully aware of the self-destructive temptation of identifying with the aggressor.

As might be expected, Memmi gives us two portraits in his book since, as he states,

> l'existence du colonialiste est trop liée à celle du colonisé, jamais il ne pourra dépasser cette dialectique. De toutes ses forces, il lui faut nier le colonisé et, en même temps, l'existence de sa victime lui est indispensable pour continuer à être. (p. 84)

A change in this structure would signify the end of colonialism, which Memmi predicts is inevitable, since the colonized cannot help but revolt against their impossible situation. I would like to concentrate on the second part of Memmi's argument here, the portrait of the colonized, in which he outlines the formation of such a creature, the offenses committed against him, his slow awakening, and the alternatives available to him. His analysis may be read at many points as a prose that parallels Césaire's poetic concerns. At other moments, the particular form of the reactions he envisions differs from Césaire's in an instructive way.

Memmi's central thesis is that the colonial structure, which is based on privilege of all kinds for the colonizer, requires the "abaissement du colonisé" to justify and perpetuate itself. The most convenient form this takes is racism, with its ensuing mythical devaluation of the other's "otherness," what he terms "le portrait-accusation" (p. 109). This myth that the colonized other is forced to inhabit is alienating, of course, since the image it projects is one of deficiency, be it moral, intellectual, cultural, or economic. And the word that recurs constantly throughout Memmi's text in analyzing the colonized is deficiency. The state of being deficient, however, is an effect and not a cause of the relationship of power. The victim has been robbed, and the perpetrator of the crime accuses him of insolvency so as to justify further exploitation. What is most important for our discussion is Memmi's investigation of the linguistic form that that robbery takes. For it is in the light of the effort at dehumanization and depersonalization that subtends the colonial dialectic that we can begin to understand how the discourse of the subject that is poetry can be a form of *engagement:*

> Le mécanisme de ce repétrissage du colonisé est lui-même éclairant.
>
> Il consiste d'abord en une série de négations. Le colonisé *n'est pas* ceci, *n'est pas* cela. Jamais il n'est considéré positivement; ou s'il l'est la qualité concédée relève d'un *manque* psychologique ou éthique. . . . Autre signe de cette dépersonnalisation du colonisé: ce que l'on pourrait appeler *la marque du plu-*

riel. Le colonisé n'est jamais caracterisé d'une manière différentielle; il n'a droit qu'à la noyade dans le collectif anonyme (*"Ils* sont ceci . . . *Ils* sont tous les mêmes.") (pp. 113–15)

And Memmi continues by demonstrating the extensive results of this kind of thinking:

Le colonisé n'est pas libre de se choisir colonisé ou non colonisé. . . . Il n'est sûrement plus un alter ego du colonisateur. C'est à peine encore un être humain. Il tend rapidement vers l'objet. . . . A l'agression idéologique qui tend à le dés-humaniser, puis à le mystifier, correspondent en somme des situations concrètes qui visent au même résultat. (pp. 115–20)

The colonized man, then, is alienated by both the superstructure and the infrastructure within the colonial situation. The worst form this alienation takes is that of depriving the colonized of the possibility of being the subject of his own history. This idea resonates strongly with Césaire's poetry. For the subject cannot appropriate its own history, whether we understand that term in a Marxist sense or in a psychoanalytic one, if it is denied the very capacity to be constituted as a subject. Colonialism attempts not only to erase the sub-ject's history, to revise it so that it seems never to have existed, but also to exclude the subject from history, which is a way of simultaneously excluding it from its potential participation in the future. Within this context, we read Césaire's poetry as an alienated subject's attempt to reinstate and reinsert itself as the subject of history. Each text constitutes an instance of the subject's his-tory. That this historicized subject is resubjected to a different alienating expe-rience, that of language, does not undermine the validity of this form of reap-propriation. The subject's colonization by language, in the case of a poet like Césaire, is at least self-imposed. For if it is true that for the subject to articu-late itself in language is already alienating, even doubly so in the context of colonialism, it also remains true that each subject can, and does, use language for itself. And although colonialism does its best not to alleviate illiteracy in the colonies, it cannot prevent the poet from saying, "I am."

Unfortunately, within the parameters of Memmi's analysis, even the state-ment "I am" is problematic, for "le colonisé n'est sauvé de l'analphabétisme que pour tomber dans le dualisme linguistique" (p. 135). This dualism is con-flictual, since the indigenous language, the one that the subject utilizes pre-cisely because of its affective charge, is devalorized in the colonial situation. One of the most ambiguous moments for the colonized man on his road to self-affirmation consists in the reclaiming of the maternal tongue and the re-jection of the usurper's language. The problem here is not one of a realistic assessment of the regenerative potential of the native tongue. It is, rather, a reactionary problem, born of protest but also blinded by protest. Here Memmi's evaluation of this specific moment in the colonial realization parallels Sartre's definition of negritude as the negative moment in a dialectical process:

> En bref, le colonisé en révolte commence par *s'accepter et se vouloir comme négativité.* . . .
>   Cette négativité, devenant un élément essentiel de sa reprise de soi et de son combat, il va l'affirmer, la glorifier jusqu'à l'absolu. . . .
>   En définitive, nous allons nous trouver en face d'une *contremythologie.* . . .
>   L'affirmation de soi du colonisé, née d'une protestation, continue à se définir par rapport à elle. En pleine révolte, le colonisé continue à penser, sentir et vivre contre et donc par rapport au colonisateur et à la colonisation. (pp. 166–67)

In other words, the revalorization of an autochthonous language risks not only being reactionary but also being condemned to remain within the confines of the colonial dialectic. If we dwell on this point, it is because of the differential light that it can shed on Césaire's specific relationship to language. Memmi, writing from, and essentially about, North Africa, is describing a valid if ambiguous linguistic choice. For Césaire, there is no language, no culture that is the equivalent of Arabic for the colonized North African. The peculiarity of colonization in the French Antilles was such that colonizer and colonized were born there together, simultaneously. To the usurpation and exploitation that characterize colonization in Africa, the history of Martinique adds the uprooting of the slaves. What cultural homogeneity there might have been within the African tribes that supplied the slave population for the Antilles had to a large extent been dispersed or dissimulated by the time it crossed the ocean. The popular local language that grew up in the islands, that is, Creole, is not the proud survivor of a once-glorious past as is Arabic or native African languages. On the contrary, it bears the mark of the master's branding iron. It is the impoverished, adulterated reflection of a more recent past, its mere existence and derivative make-up bearing witness to the cultural dissipation and castration effected by slavery. This, of course, does not signify that it is completely devoid of its own history, folklore, or affect. It only means that its scope is so circumscribed that its revival has never been an option for Césaire, though it has been for others. Césaire's position is therefore paradigmatic, absolute. We emphasize this because it is essential to understand to what extent Césaire's cultural situation forces him into a radical position vis-à-vis the French language. There is no reactionary alternative for him in language. This is not to say that nostalgia is absent from his poetry. On the contrary, it is the absence we sense everywhere in his poetry. But being a nostal-

gia for a plenitude that never was, for Sartre's "Afrique fantôme," it links his
poetry far more closely to that radical, self-conscious current in modern poetry that practices language as an approximation of absence than to the absence of literature in Creole. In the poem entitled "Nocturne d'une nostalgie,"
for example, repetition is used to render absence present in a self-perpetuating
structure whereby the nostalgia of the title can be nothing more than a desire
for the repetition of absence.[6]

Césaire himself has declared in numerous interviews that French has always been his language and that there has never been a question for him of
writing in any other.[7] One might raise the question in passing of whether such
a statement is indicative of the ultimate cultural alienation and impoverish-
ment that France has wrought in the Antilles. Césaire does not live his relationship to French in that way, however, as we shall see. Even when he
founded the review *Tropiques* with René Ménil and Suzanne Césaire in 1941,
the specific purpose of which was to reaffirm Antillean cultural values, using
Creole as an alternative language was not a real option for him.

This leads us to the last point in Memmi's argument that will be discussed
here, the untenable position of the colonized writer, his drama, as Memmi
puts it. He is caught between Scylla and Charibdis:

> . . . Pour qui écrirait-il, pour quel public? S'il s'obstine à écrire dans sa
> langue, il se condamne à parler devant un auditoire de sourds. Le peuple est
> inculte et ne lit aucune langue. . . . Une seule issue lui reste: qu'il écrive dans la
> langue du colonisateur. . . .
> Curieux destin que d'écrire pour un autre peuple que le sien! Plus curieux
> encore que d'écrire pour les vainqueurs de son peuple! (pp. 137–38)

Although the ambiguity of the writer's position within the colonial framework is correctly analyzed by Memmi, and manifests itself even in Césaire,
albeit in a quite different form, Memmi's polarization of the two options is
somewhat naive, and he seems curiously unaware of his own situation as a
colonized writer and of his motivation for choosing the French language.
Might we not infer that he himself is caught up in the dialectic that he de-

6. Aimé Césaire, *Ferrements* (Paris: Editions du Seuil, 1960), p. 20.
7. See, for example, this excerpt from a recent "Entretien avec Aimé Césaire" by
Jacqueline Leiner which serves as an introduction to the reedition of *Tropiques,*
pp. x–xiv: "On a toujours besoin de prendre conscience de soi. Mais ni Ménil ni moi,
n'aurions été capables de l'écrire en créole. . . . Ce que nous avions à dire, je ne sais
même pas si c'est formulable en créole. . . . Pour moi, l'écriture est liée au français,
et pas au créole, c'est tout. . . . Ah, moi, je ne suis pas prisonnier de la langue
française!"

scribes in such a way that prevents him from imagining a synthesis even as he already practices it? For the conclusions that he draws from the difficulty of the writer's position not only cannot account for Césaire's particular subjective solution to the problem; they also, paradoxically, seem to eliminate the possibility of his own engaged book:

> Le problème ne peut se clore que de deux manières: par tarissement naturel de la littérature colonisée; les prochaines générations, nées dans la liberté, écriront spontanément dans leur langue retrouvée. Sans attendre si loin, une autre possibilité peut tenter l'écrivain; décider d'appartenir totalement à la littérature métropolitaine. . . . C'est alors le suicide de la littérature colonisée. Dans les deux perspectives, seule l'échéance différant, la littérature colonisée de langue européenne semble condamnée à mourir jeune. (p. 140)

This kind of writing is an excellent example of that dual, imaginary thought, weighted with ethical connotations, that Fredric Jameson scrutinizes admirably in his essay that will be discussed at the end of this chapter. Caught between the concepts of a good language and a bad language, Memmi is blind to the very lesson of his own seminal book and is forced to ignore history. History has so far proved his conclusions wrong. In the 1960s and the 1970s, the years of massive decolonization, there was a flourishing of colonized literature in both French and English. Although the reason may seem obvious, it must be stated. The question is not that of a choice between writing in a "good" or "bad" language but rather that of the way in which the language is appropriated and problematized, and to what extent the author is self-aware as a producer, as Walter Benjamin would say. Memmi's text is exemplary. Although it is written in French, or because it is written in French, in classically lucid French prose, moreover, its denunciatory power is enormous. It is an attack from "within." And while it may attest to the pervasive, successful dissemination of the French language in the colonies more than to anything else, the book has been read widely by those "without." It is an undeniable reality, for better or for worse, that French (and/or English) is the lingua franca for those colonies that stretch from the Caribbean to Africa to the Indian Ocean to Southeast Asia.

The third alternative, one that offers the colonized writer a means of resolving his ambiguous position, and one that Memmi and Césaire both have recourse to, albeit in very different discourses, is to utilize the "appareil-à-penser de l'ennemi" against the enemy.

In his preface to the 1966 edition of the *Portrait du colonisé*, Memmi becomes a reader of his own text, and the rhetoric he uses places him and his text within the problematic of *engagement* as we understand it throughout this study, namely, as an attempt to articulate a relationship between the particular and the general, where the general is split into either collective alter ego or collective enemy, for the purposes of transforming that relationship:

> Bref, j'ai entrepris cet inventaire de la condition du Colonisé d'abord pour me comprendre moi-même et identifier ma place au milieu des autres hommes. Ce furent mes lecteurs, qui étaient loin d'être tous des Tunisiens, qui m'ont convaincu plus tard que ce Portrait était également le leur. (p. 11)

Since we are generally less concerned here with a committed intention or motivation than with the production of a text, a final remark of Memmi's, again illuminated by hindsight, should be added. For he sees his text as a moment of reflection, mirroring not only his own concerns but also those of all the protagonists involved:

> Mais je commençais à entrevoir, . . . de quel appoint pouvait être, pour des hommes en lutte, la simple description, mais rigoureuse, ordonnée de leurs misères, de leur humiliation et de leur condition objective d'opprimé. Et combien explosive pouvait être la révélation à la conscience claire du colonisé comme du colonisateur, d'une situation explosive par nature. (p. 13)

He does admit, then, retroactively, to the subversive potential of a text that, one might argue, was written for the enemy or, at least, in the enemy's language. But the rhetoric of this passage implies Memmi's belief that language is transparent, that it becomes explosive as what is seen through it is explosive. Césaire, on the other hand, as a poet, has a different conception of how he must utilize the "appareil-à-penser de l'ennemi." He envisions the attack as coming from within—indeed, he declares himself to be a poetic son of Mallarmé—but he transcends Memmi's conceptualization of the role of the colonized writer in that he sees the very use of language as the battleground of liberation:

> Seulement, j'essaie, j'ai toujours voulu *infléchir* le français. Ainsi, si j'ai beaucoup aimé Mallarmé, c'est parce que j'ai compris à travers lui, que la langue, au fond, est arbitraire. . . .
> Mon effort a été d'infléchir le français, de le transformer pour exprimer, disons: "ce moi, ce moi-nègre, ce moi-créole, ce moi-martiniquais, ce moi-antillais." C'est pour cela que je me suis beaucoup plus intéressé à la poésie qu'à la prose, et ce *dans la mesure où c'est le poète qui fait son langage*. Alors que, en général, le prosateur se sert du langage.[8]

Césaire's poetic discourse diverges, necessarily, from Memmi's expository prose. Yet the latter's work, as an outline of the injustices and imbalances in

---

8. Ibid., p. xiv.

the colonial dialectic that demand transformation, serves as a useful thematization of Césaire's point of departure.

When we approach the works of Frantz Fanon, we are coming closer to Césaire's world and to the complex fabric woven by the relationship of the writing subject to a politically committed text. In many ways, the form and evolution of Fanon's thought, as presented in his two major books, *Peau noire, masques blancs,* and *Les Damnés de la terre,* offer striking parallels to Césaire's. In the interstices between the two men's texts, I shall outline the ways in which they inform each other. Like Césaire, Fanon was a black man from Martinique. Like Césaire, Fanon's intellectual commitment was to reveal the history of the speaking subject in an alienated context, and he began with himself, writing what might be called a psychoautobiography in *Peau noire,* the articulation of which owes much to the groundwork that Césaire laid in the *Cahier.* And like Césaire, when the subject exposed an oppressed and conflicted situation, Fanon called for its transcendence and transformation, which required a reversal of the existing colonial values. Unlike Césaire, however, Fanon left Martinique to become a revolutionary in Algeria. Césaire chose to become politically active at home. It is not the purpose here to speculate on the lives or the choices of these two writers, but a rich comparison obtains if we imagine Fanon's geographical expansion to Africa as analogous to the evolution of the spatialization of Césaire's text when he moved from poetry to the theater in the 1960s.

There is an intertextual relationship of reciprocal transcendence between the works of Fanon and Césaire. The early Fanon was an avid reader of Césaire, and *Peau noire* articulates many of the same community of problems as the *Cahier,* albeit from a different point of articulation. Moreover, as a reading of both psychoanalytic and philosophical texts, including those of Lacan, Hegel, and Sartre that deal with an alienated consciousness, *Peau noire* functions as an informative critical model of the problematic of *engagement* and the language of the subject. The rhetoric of this text is that which Fanon defines as the committed style in *Les Damnés de la terre:*

> Ainsi s'explique suffisamment le style des intellectuels colonisés qui décident d'exprimer cette phase de la conscience en train de se libérer. Style heurté, fortement imagé car l'image est le pont-levis qui permet aux énergies inconscientes de s'éparpiller dans les prairies environnantes. Style nerveux, animé de rythmes de part en part habité par une vie éruptive. Coloré aussi, bronzé, ensoleillé et violent. Ce style, . . . n'est point comme on a bien voulu le dire un caractère racial mais traduit avant tout un corps à corps, révèle la nécessité dans laquelle s'est trouvé cet homme de se faire mal, de saigner réellement de sang rouge, de se libérer d'une partie de son être qui déjà renfermait des germes de pourriture. Combat douloureux, rapide où immanquablement le muscle devait se substituer au concept. (*Les Damnés,* p. 152)

The violent, oppositional character of this style derives, in part at least, from the contradictory nature of the project that is Fanon's book. It is an attempt to identify the black-white relationship as it obtains in the Antilles by means of a psychoanalytic interpretation of inferiority and superiority complexes. This interpretation implies a recognition of the subject, the individual, the particular. And yet, says Fanon:

> . . . Il demeure toutefois évident que pour nous la désaliénation du Noir implique une prise de conscience abrupte des réalités économiques et sociales. S'il y a complexe d'infériorité, c'est à la suite d'un double processus:
> —économique d'abord;
> —par intériorisation, ou mieux, épidermisation de cette infériorité, ensuite. . . . A côté de la phylogénie et de l'ontogénie, il y a sociogénie. (*Peau noire,* p. 8)

Fanon is also a reader of Jung. For he investigates the concept of the collective unconscious in an effort to mediate between the particular and the general, only to conclude that the notion, as well, is culturally determined. At the heart of Fanon's difficulty in delimiting his subject and grasping it conceptually lies his own admittedly ambivalent attitude toward the idea of race, which, for my purposes here, I shall equate with negritude. Like Césaire, Fanon as writing subject is striving toward the human, the universal, but the resistance he encounters from the (white) other forces him back onto an exploration of his black identity. Chapter 5 of *Peau noire,* entitled "L'expérience vécue du noir," is Fanon's first-person, subjective account of a black man's alienation and his various attempts at disalienation, ranging from a desire to identify with the aggressor, to the wish to hide, to the need to assume his black past as a source of pride, to the analysis of the myth of the black man as the incarnation of a terrifying sexuality. The alienation is articulated in terms of the Sartrian dialectic of otherness as it is expounded in *Réflexions sur la question juive* and *L'Être et le néant.* It is in discovering his *être-pour-autrui,* when he encounters the white man, that Fanon is forced to explore the shame and the contempt of self and, simultaneously, to transcend them. It is important to note here that for passages at a time, Fanon substitutes Césaire's voice for his own. Parts of the *Cahier* are quoted at length, not as illustrations but as identifications. Fanon reads the convolutions in the trajectory of Césaire's subject as his own, and the identification permits him to assume his own *négritude:*

> Et voici le nègre réhabilité, "debout à la barre," gouvernant le monde de son intuition, le nègre retrouvé, ramassé, revendiqué, assumé, et c'est un nègre, non pas, ce n'est point un nègre, mais le nègre, alertant les antennes fécondes du monde, planté dans l'avant-scène du monde, aspergeant le monde de sa puissance poétique, "poreux à tous les souffles du monde." J'épouse le monde! Je

suis le monde! Le Blanc n'a jamais compris cette substitution magique. Le Blanc veut le monde; . . . Il l'asservit. (*Peau noire*, p. 103)

Césaire's will to speak for others is validated by this kind of awakening. The quotations in the passage above are taken from the *Cahier*. Yet no sooner does Fanon appropriate his negritude, an attitude he arrives at by utilizing the tools of Sartre's phenomenological analysis of alienation, than he finds Sartre reemerging as the enemy, the "other." Sartre says in *L'Être et le néant*, "autrui me vole mon monde." Fanon would now say, "Sartre me vole ma négritude." He quotes Sartre's argument to the effect that negritude is the antithetical moment in a dialectic that must be surpassed, and that we discussed earlier in this chapter. Fanon's reaction is violent:

> Et quand j'essayais, sur le plan de l'idée et de l'activité intellectuelle, de revendiquer ma négritude, on me l'arrachait, on me démontrait que ma démarche n'était qu'un terme dans la dialectique. . . .
> Quand je lus cette page, je sentais qu'on me volait ma dernière chance. . . . Au moment où je tente une saisie de mon être, Sartre, qui demeure l'Autre, en me nommant m'enlève toute illusion. Alors que je lui dis: "Ma Négritude n'est ni une tour ni une cathédrale" alors que moi, au paroxysme du vécu et de la fureur, je proclame cela, il me rappelle que ma négritude n'est qu'un temps faible. En vérité, en vérité, je vous dis, mes épaules ont glissé de la structure du monde, mes pieds n'ont plus senti la caresse du sol. Sans passé nègre, sans avenir nègre, il m'était impossible d'exister ma négrerie. (*Peau noire*, pp. 107–12)

Fanon is describing exactly that existential nausea that Sartre made famous. He faults Sartre with failing to perceive that for the black man, the white is not only the other but also, always, the master, and the very hold that Sartre's conceptual models have on Fanon's thought testifies to this ambiguous influence. His dialectical relationship to Sartre is a personal one and not merely an intellectual one. It dramatizes exactly what is being thematized. Sartre has the power to disregard Fanon's newly won identity. This structure refers us, in turn, to Fanon's reading of the Hegelian dialectic of the Master and the Slave from *The Phenomenology of Mind:* The other is endowed with the power to confer recognition on me. This is a reciprocal relationship, according to Hegel. But Fanon emphasizes the difference between Hegel's master and the colonial one:

> . . . Ici le maître se moque de la conscience de l'esclave. Il ne réclame pas la reconnaissance de ce dernier. . . . De même, l'esclave ici n'est nullement assimilable à celui qui, se perdant dans l'objet, trouve dans le travail la source de sa libération. Le nègre veut être comme le maître. Ainsi est-il moins indépendant que l'esclave hégélien. . . .

> Ici, l'esclave se tourne vers le maître et abandonne l'objet. (*Peau noire,*
> p. 179n)

Once again, the black man is thrown back onto his specificity. This constant tension, which motivates the subject toward the other only to force it back onto itself with a new awareness of that subject's constitution, is typical of the *Cahier,* too, as we shall see in chapter 2. How does Fanon break out of this vicious circle? Continuing to admit the subject's need for recognition by the other as constitutive of its self-consciousness, he makes the point that the historical liberation of the slaves cannot be defined as that recognition, since it was imposed from without. The other must constantly be perceived as opposed to the black subject, thereby awakening its desire for freedom by recognition and its will to die, if necessary, for the fulfillment of this desire:

> "C'est seulement par le risque de sa vie qu'on conserve la liberté." . . . Ce
> risque signifie que je dépasse la vie vers un bien suprême qui est la transforma-
> tion en vérité objective universellement valable de la certitude subjective que
> j'ai de ma propre valeur. (*Peau noire,* p. 177)

Once again, the ever present vocabulary of a passage from individual to general haunts Fanon's writing. This quotation is found in the concluding pages of *Peau noire,* and we might construe it as the author's adieu to the native land, both literally and figuratively. For the "bien suprême" that he will embrace from now on, the transcending object investment that will become his work and his discourse, is the revolution. This transformation can be seen in the very titles of his works, *Peau noire, masques blancs* being the individual black man's coming-to-consciousness of the "certitude subjective que j'ai de ma propre valeur," and *Les Damnés de la terre,* being an analysis, a critique, and a program for transforming this new consciousness into a global value. This substitution cannot be effected without a confrontation, according to the rules of the colonial dialectic. And it is not surprising that the first chapter of *Les Damnés de la terre* is entitled "De la violence." The justification is clear: the colonial situation was engendered through violence, therefore it can by defeated only by an equal and opposite reaction, that is, more violence. We recognize echoes of Memmi here. Although Fanon would claim that violence is action, and therefore freedom, its conceptualization implies reaction as well, which identifies it as remaining within the colonial parameters, still defined by the actions of the other. There is further evidence for this complication in what we see as a certain violence that Fanon perpetrates on himself. Ironically, he has introjected Sartre, perhaps in spite of himself, in his attempt to mediate between the individual and the collective and repudiates negritude as the same "temps faible," the same negative moment in a dialectical progression, which we found in "Orphée noir":

En Afrique, la littérature colonisée des vingt dernières années n'est pas une littérature nationale mais une littérature de nègres. Le concept de négritude par exemple était l'antithèse affective sinon logique de cette insulte que l'homme blanc faisait à l'humanité. . . . A l'affirmation inconditionelle de la culture européenne a succédé l'affirmation inconditionnelle de la culture africaine. Dans l'ensemble les chantres de la négritude opposeront la vieille Europe à la jeune Afrique, la raison ennuyeuse à la poésie, la logique oppressive à la piaffante nature, d'un côté raideur, cérémonie, protocole, scepticisme, de l'autre, ingénuité, pétulance, liberté, pourquoi pas luxuriance? Mais aussi irresponsabilité. (*Les Damnés,* p. 146)

Why is negritude irresponsible for Fanon? On the one hand, it is regressive, bypassing the demands of the present in order to revalorize the past. On the other hand, it is too general. Because of its racial quality, its appeal to all people of color threatens to dilute the strength of that revolution that must bring about each individual nation's liberation. However, Fanon has not forgotten his own roots or his own position as an intellectual. His critique of negritude is more subtle, motivated from within as well as by theory. And it is here that he can again illuminate some of the complexities in Césaire's position.

Fanon enumerates three phases in the evolution of the colonized writer. The first he terms assimilationist and imitative. The next two are of particular interest to our exploration of the relationship between *engagement* and the language of the subject:

Dans un deuxième temps le colonisé est ébranlé et décide de se souvenir. Cette période de création correspond approximativement à la replongée que nous venons de décrire. Mais comme le colonisé n'est pas inséré dans son peuple, comme il entretient des relations d'extériorité avec son peuple, il se contente de souvenir. Période d'angoisse, de malaise, expérience de la mort, expérience aussi de la nausée. . . .

Enfin dans une troisième période, dite de combat, le colonisé après avoir tenté de se perdre dans le peuple, de se perdre avec le peuple, va au contraire, secouer le peuple . . . il se transforme en réveilleur de peuple. Littérature de combat, littérature révolutionnaire, littérature nationale. (*Les Damnés,* pp. 153–54)

These last two stages could easily be used to describe Fanon's own project as it evolves in the two works under discussion here. But they are also applicable to Césaire's poetry, with this difference: these attitudes exist simultaneously. There are instances of merging, of isolation, of individuation, often within the same poetic text. Like the word "nègre" in the poem "Mot," the subject seems to have been born "tout armé." [9] The clear temporal evolution that Fanon outlines is somewhat simplistic in comparison with the density of

9. See chapter 4, "The Subject and Negritude."

subjective articulations in any one of Césaire's poems. In "Hors des jours étrangers," for example, we shall see that it is through the subject's desire to "secouer le peuple" that the threat of its exteriority to this desire is revealed.[10] All of the oppositions that structure Fanon's work come face to face with each other anew in the Césairian text. And the relationship between the individual and the collective, whether posed thematically or rhetorically, is often made more problematical, dramatized as inadequate, than resolved or synthesized.

Negritude, which Fanon comes to understand finally as too amorphous a concept, is Césaire's hope of mediating between the subject and the people. National liberation, Fanon's aspiration for a rehumanization of the colonized, calls for a peculiar kind of reparticularization of the general where the individual will be gratified as a result of bringing about a new sociopolitical order. Fanon's prose allows itself to wander over entire intellectual continents, from the realms of political history to psychiatric case studies, from literary criticism to psychological and anthropological essays, from phenomenology to existentialism, from negritude to Marxism, from Martinique to Algeria to Indochina to the newly decolonized African states. Yet this intellectual liberty represents a luxury that the poetic form Césaire chooses does not afford. The poem, in its "islandness," is a figure for the decision to stay, to forge something different from within, to battle the desire to branch out as well as the desire to be rooted, on home turf, as it were, to substitute the subject for alienation. This difference does not mean that Césaire is blinded either to the exemplary nature of Fanon's project or to the difficulties of his own. As the subject of the *Cahier* presented the early Fanon with a mirror image that facilitated his assuming of his blackness, so Fanon's model offers Césaire a similar yet different reflection against which he can define himself. In delineating the other, one also comments on the self. This is nowhere more evident than in Césaire's "Hommage à Frantz Fanon," where he reads Fanon's life and texts as interchangeable:

> Fanon mort, on peut méditer sa vie: son côté épique, son côté tragique, aussi.
> L'épique est que Fanon a vécu jusqu'au bout de son destin de paladin de la liberté, et a dominé de si haut son particularisme humain qu'il est mort un soldat de l'universel.
> Le tragique? C'est que sans doute cet Antillais n'aura pas trouvé des Antilles à sa taille et d'avoir été, parmi les siens, un solitaire.
> Peut-être Fanon n'est-il monté si haut et n'a-t-il vu si large que parce que Antillais, c'est-à-dire parti de si bas et d'une base si étroite. Peut-être fallait-il être Antillais, c'est-à-dire si dénué, si dépersonnalisé pour partir avec une telle fougue à la conquête de soi et de la plénitude; Antillais, enfin, pour vouloir,

10. See chapter 5, "The Subject and *Engagement*."

avec une telle force échapper à l'impuissance par l'action et à la solitude par la fraternité. (p. 121)

These words are so moving because they describe both the subject writing and the subject written about. There is an extraordinary complementarity between the two. And yet, in René Char's terms, Fanon's is a research from the summit, Césaire's from the base. Césaire's poetic discourse is by no means removed from this same Antillean reality. However, it functions as a means of stripping it bare, paring it down to the essential and awful truth of that reality. This is what provides many of the poems with their powerful negative capability. The words do not describe; they show themselves in the act of chiseling away. In the poem "Comptine," for example, the luxurious rhythms, alliterations, and rhymes of the opening verses give way, gradually, to the exigencies imposed by a violent reality:

C'est cette mince pellicule sur le remous du vin mal déposé de la mer
c'est ce grand cabrement des chevaux de la terre arrêtés à la dernière seconde
    sur un sursaut du gouffre
c'est ce sable noir que se saboule au hoquet de l'abîme

. . . .
ce rapt
ce sac
ce vrac

cette terre[11]

The text challenges and transforms itself from within. This is Césaire's particular poetic approach to his situation. One might say that he breaks out of these confines by turning to the theater. But we read it more as a multiplication of the subject and a dramatization of the subject's matter than as a qualitative modulation to another genre. Even Césaire's theater remains as a confrontation of that tragic solitude of the engaged subject with its inadequate object which Césaire ascribes to Fanon's life and work.

UNLIKE the works of the three authors we have just examined, Fredric Jameson's article "Imaginary and Symbolic in Lacan: Marxism, Psychoanalytic Criticism, and the Problem of the Subject" does not address itself specifically to the colonial situation. But the nature of its subject provides an essential means of mediating between this chapter and the textual readings that constitute the remainder of this book. For the problematic that structures our readings, that of the relationship between the social and political concept of *engagement* and

11. Césaire, *Ferrements,* pp. 8–9.

the subjective discourse of poetry, is treated in a different way in Jameson's essay. As Jameson states in his introduction: "The attempt to coordinate a Marxist and a Freudian criticism confronts . . . a dilemma . . . that of the insertion of the subject, or, in a different terminology the difficulty of providing mediation between social phenomena and what must be called private, rather than even merely individual facts" (p. 338).

The common denominator that obtains between psychoanalysis and poetry is that they both elaborate a discourse of the subject. Discourse, whether the language of case history or that of literature, is the most basic of social phenomena, yet the process by which the subject constitutes itself, socializes itself in discourse, is a problematic one, since in its passage from the particular to the universal, it undergoes various stages of alienation from itself. In Jameson's lucid exposition of the Lacanian orders of the Imaginary, the Symbolic, and the Real, it becomes clear to what extent Lacan's relational mappings of the subject can help account for the difficulties we encounter in reading Césaire's poetry. For when we speak of *engagement* in connection with poetry, we are speaking of ideology, in the sense of the Lacanian-inspired definition of that term given by Althusser: "The 'representation' of the Imaginary relationship of individuals to their Real conditions of existence." Jameson extends this definition by making ideology "the place of the insertion of the subject in those realms or orders—the Symbolic . . . the Real . . . both of which radically transcend individual experience in their very structure" (p. 394). He further equates Lacan's Real with history, thereby demonstrating that for both psychoanalysis and Marxism, the concept of the referent cannot be eliminated too easily. This has far-reaching implications for Césaire. For while it may seem simplistic to state that a corpus that we designate as politically committed must, by definition, account for the colonial referent against which it opposes itself, the problem becomes infinitely more interesting when we realize how the textual representations of the subject's relationship to this referent can be read as various instances of transformative participation in each of the discontinuous Lacanian orders.

Furthermore, Lacan's spatial mappings of the decentered subject shed light on Césaire's own topologies, not only those of the poetic text's spatialization, the relationship of the signifiers' black islandness to the white sea of the page, but also, as we shall see, those of the geographic colonial triangle, France, Martinique, and Africa. The subject appears textually as marginal to, confined within, decentered by, freed from one or more of the points of the triangle, according to the problems articulated by each text.

In Césaire's poetry, the subject is often constituted by the oppositional relationship that the text posits to the (colonial) other, the enemy, which oppresses, victimizes, inhibits, or alienates. This duality is the essence of the

Imaginary. In his reading of Lacan's "mirror stage," Jameson notes that it defines "a kind of situational experience of otherness as pure relationship, as struggle, violence, and antagonism" (p. 356). Given the dynamics of the colonial situation as it was outlined in the texts discussed, we should not be surprised when we encounter these oppositional structures over and over in Césaire's poems. We are not speaking of symbols here, as Kesteloot does, but rather of a function. In the colonial context, the Imaginary relationship is reciprocal, the colonialist having first entertained an Imaginary relationship to the colonized, naming him as the bad other. Either protagonist is designated by Jameson's definition:

> The Imaginary may thus be described as a peculiar spatial configuration, whose bodies primarily entertain relationships of inside/outside with one another, which is then traversed and reorganized by that primordial rivalry and transitivistic substitution of imagoes, that indistinction of primary narcissism and aggressivity, from which our later conceptions of good and evil derive. This stage is already an alienation. (p. 357)

This reciprocity of the Imaginary relationship accounts for the analyses of Sartre, Memmi, and Fanon. While all three are aware that, on some level, continuing to represent this relationship in Imaginary terms condemns the committed writer to remaining locked within the colonial dialectic, they would also argue that because the relationship was inherent in the situation from its inception, restating it from the oppressed point of view is the first step toward breaking out of it. We see this as a possible answer to Jameson's implied critique of this kind of analysis:

> This approach—the reading of cultural phenomena in terms of otherness—derives from the dialectic of the relationship to the Other in Sartre's *Being and Nothingness*, and, beyond that, from the Hegelian account of the Master and the Slave in the *Phenomenology*. It is a dialectic which . . . seemed to lay the basis for an aggressive critique of the relations of domination: hence . . . its extension by Frantz Fanon to the whole realm of Third World Theory and of the psychopathology of the colonized and the colonial other; and something just like a theory of otherness must surely always be implicit in a politics which for whatever reason substitutes categories of race for those of class, and the struggle for colonial independence for that of the class struggle proper. (pp. 379–80)

To return to Césaire, there is a derivative form of the Imaginary relationship in which the role of the other is played not by the colonialist but, rather, by that closer alter ego, the brother, the comrade, the people. This is particularly evident in Césaire's plays, where a visionary hero is pitted against a reluctant, passive, or even hostile community. Yet it is impossible for the subject to represent their alienation without being implicated in that image to the extent that the subject is identified with it. Hence the rage, despair, and disgust of some of the poems, on the one hand, and, on the other, either the projective utopianism of the future tense or the search for consensual validation in a revalorization of the past. When the subject is thus trapped in this unavoidable but undesirable dual relationship with what should be the equivalent of itself, it is easy to see how the introduction of the colonialist other, the "real" enemy, provides a means of modulating to a different order of alienation, more abstract in some ways, and freed from the uncomfortable constraints of being "too close to home." This is analogous to Jameson's affirmation that "the Symbolic Order (or language itself) restructures the Imaginary by introducing a third term into the hitherto infinite regression of the duality of the latter's mirror images" (pp. 383–84).

Yet in acceding to the Symbolic Order, that is, in constituting itself in language, the subject encounters new forms of alienation. Jameson outlines three groups within the Symbolic where the subject's linguistic alienation is particularly visible: the naming function of language, the representation of the subject in language by the signifier of the personal pronoun, with its concomitant repression of "the real subject," and the alienation by the Other, be it other people or the signifier itself.

I propose as a working hypothesis here that the Césairian poetic subject, permeated as it necessarily must be by the duality of the colonial situation, entertains an Imaginary relationship even to these forms of its own alienation by the Symbolic. Two obvious but important remarks must be added in connection with this conjecture. First, in discussing the distance that derives between the subject and its image in the "mirror stage," Jameson gives weight to the "psychic function of narrative and fantasy in the attempts of the subject to reintegrate his or her alienated image" (p. 353). Second, despite Césaire's objections that French has always been his first and only language, if we accept the Lacanian notion that the subject undergoes alienation from itself when it is assumed into the Symbolic Order, we can only conclude that this alienation must be heightened by the exteriority of the colonial language. The textual support for this inference comes to us through the oppositional relationship that can be detected throughout the poetry between the subject and the naming function of language. Not only are the texts punctuated by specific references to the Antillean flora and fauna that exclude the other; they are also full of neologisms, archaisms, and esoteric or recherché technical vocabulary that are, we might say, more-French-than-French and that transcend the other by beating him at his own game. One could argue that their presence as a reaction to the alienating powers of the enemy's signifier serves only to reinforce that alienation. We would tend, rather, to agree with Jameson that "The relationship of the literary text to its image content is thus . . . not that of the production of imagery, but rather of its mastery and control" (p. 376).

The Césairian subject's attempts at disalienation through the mastering of the master's language and the rivalrous reappropriation of the naming function of language lead us to posit an analogous oppositional relationship with regard to the alienating representation of the subject by the personal pronoun and to what Roman Jakobson defines as "la fonction poétique." Let us juxtapose these two ideas. First, Lacan's, as expounded by Anika Rifflet-Lemaire: "The subject mediated by language is irremediably divided because it has been excluded from the symbolic chain [the lateral relations of signifiers among themselves] at the very moment at which it became represented in it." Second, Jakobson's, quoted from the chapter "Linguistique et poétique" in his *Essais de linguistique générale:* "La fonction poétique projette le principe d'équivalence de l'axe de la sélection sur l'axe de la combinaison." [12] It is clear, of course, that Jakobson is describing a structuring element by which poetry is defined and not some phenomenological subject writing poetry. But poetry provides a privileged corpus for the alienated subject in that the signifying chain is constructed according to the laws of selection derived in ordinary language from the realm of paradigm. What are we saying if not that the signifying chain in poetry, ruled by the principle of equivalence (which is itself oppositional), affords the alienated subject a unique opportunity for substitutive investment from which it is usually barred by the function of the symbolic chain in language generally? It follows that poetry is revelatory of that unconscious desire of the subject that is alienated and repressed in language.

As for the Imaginary relationship of the Césairian poetic subject to that third alienating aspect of the Symbolic Order, namely, the Other, we can best see it at work in our analysis of the poem "Mot," in the chapter on "The Subject and Negritude."

It remains for us, then, in following Jameson's argument, to map the poetic representation of the subject's relationship to the Real. If we agree with Jameson to equate the Real with history, we see that it, too, threatens more often than not to break down into a binary opposition between good history and bad history, between that often glorified but never-more-to-be-coincided-with pre-individualistic moment of the African past, on the one hand, and the still present but alienating (and therefore, also, never-to-be-coincided-with) colo-

12. Anika Rifflet-Lemaire, *Jacques Lacan* (Brussels: Dessart, 1970), quoted in Jameson, "Imaginary and Symbolic in Lacan," p. 363; Roman Jakobson, *Essais de linguistique générale*, p. 220.

nial past on the other. Both are reconstituted in some form or another in Césaire's poetry, but whether alone or together they are insufficient to "embody
the 'truth' of the subject" (p. 389).

In tracing the "theme of the subject" as it appears in contemporary schools
of critical thought, particularly those of the Frankfurt School and of the *Tel
Quel* group, Jameson affirms that "in Marxism as well as in psychoanalysis
there is a problem—even a crisis of the subject" (p. 390). While the fate of
the subject as outlined by these various analyses is not particularly applicable
to our problematic, Jameson's conclusions concerning them are: "The solution can only lie, it seems to me, in the renewal of Utopian thinking, of creative speculation as to the place of the subject at the other end of historical
time, in a social order which has put behind it class organization, commodity
production and the market, alienated labor, and the implacable determinism
of an historical logic beyond the control of humanity" (p. 393).

It is important to bear in mind, as we proceed now to our textual readings
in the hope of defining the relationship between *engagement* and the language
of the subject in Césaire's poetry, that Jameson conceives of the "Lacanian
doctrine of the decentered subject—particularly insofar as that structural
'subversion' of the subject aims, not at renunciation or repression, but rather
precisely at the realization of desire—as a model for a theoretical elaboration
of an ideology of the collective" (p. 395).

Poetry is praxis, of course, not theory. But Césaire's poetic praxis can be
read more fully in the light of Jameson's instructive models for mediating between Marx and Lacan. In Césaire's poems the reader is confronted again and
again with a projected utopian future. Moreover, the very articulation of the
poem becomes the place of the subject's desired insertion in the collective
realm of the Symbolic or the Real. Jameson helps us to understand that this
insertion may define the impossible, alienating distance between the subject
and its desired *engagement*.

2. The Subject of the *Cahier*

Mon nom: offensé; mon prénom: humilié; mon état: ré-
volté; mon âge: l'âge de la pierre.

Aimé Césaire,
Et les chiens se taisaient

CRITICS HAVE attempted, with varying degrees of success, to pinpoint the
exact moment and locus of the writing of the *Cahier d'un retour au pays
natal,* in what seems to be a misguided effort to account for the temporal and
spatial complexities of the poem.[1] A good case in point is the following passage by Thomas Hale, from his article entitled "Structural Dynamics in a
Third World Classic: Aimé Césaire's *Cahier d'un retour au pays natal*":

> Until recently, *Cahier d'un retour au pays natal* has been regarded as the prod-
> uct of nostalgia and melancholy, as something jotted down hastily on the eve of
> the poet's return to Martinique after eight long years in Paris. But this view does
> not account for the extreme sharpness and intensity of the images which portray
> the island. . . . If we now know that Césaire returned to Martinique in 1936 for
> a summer vacation, then it becomes apparent that much of the first part of the
> poem is based not on the distant memories of a *lycée* student . . . but springs
> instead from the immediate, fresh and often shocking impressions of a man who
> rediscovers his country for the first time with a more mature vision. . . .
>   This experienced return to his native land produces . . . a desire to flee the
> island and rejoin instead the larger world of the 1930's. . . . Only after he has
> returned to Europe, a return which remains fairly obscure in the text, is the nar-
> rator able to project a second return to Martinique, a return which, this time, he
> will effect in his imagination. (pp. 166–67)

While these facts about the history of the writing of the *Cahier* may indeed
be true, the literalness of their referential concerns inhibits them from dealing
with the structural dynamics within the text itself. They cannot account for the
rich tensions that obtain in the realities of exile/return, alienation/identifica-
tion, subject/object, descent/aspiration. Nor can such a reading provide insight into the way Césaire's obsessive metaphors function in the text, particu-

1. Aimé Césaire, *Cahier d'un retour au pays natal,* trans. Emile Snyder, bilingual
ed., preface by André Breton, 3d ed. (Paris: Présence Africaine, 1971). References to
Cahier d'un retour au pays natal are included in the text.

29

larly that pervasive figure which we shall call "islandness." This "islandness" has enormous value for the subject, both rhetorically and structurally. It is separation, difference, delimitation, self-enclosure, and, by extension, self-imposed constraint. This last definition relates it to poetic form itself. Geography, identity, and writing are intertwined throughout Césaire's poetry.

A different model is clearly required, then, one that would allow us to read the *Cahier* and account for its structural dynamics from the inside. The difficulties of the text must be problematized as diacritical tools rather than skirted as obstacles to imposing an interpretation. The problematic of the politically engaged writing subject places us at the center of the text's complexities. We have only to examine the title of the poem to realize that the definition of the subject, what Sartre would call its existential project, cannot be separated from the writing project. "Cahier" denotes a writing-exercise book, connotes a private, reflexive, for-the-self aspect, and also sensitizes us to the presence of a split subject: the subject represented in the text and the biographical subject, Césaire.

We shall attempt to show to what extent identity is linked to the poetic praxis throughout the *Cahier*. In fact, it can be read as a dual apprenticeship in a common project, a coming-into-being-of-the-subject-as-writer, not unlike that of Proust's *A la recherche du temps perdu*. It is useful to pause for a moment at this comparison of the two titles. The "Cahier d'un retour" corresponds to "A la recherche" in nature. The form, the scope, the themes, are of course different, but the project is similar. The repetitive potential implied in "un retour," as well as its quality of quest, is contained equally in "la recherche" and "temps perdu." The comparison bears more fruit if we consider that the nominal object of Proust's quest is "temps perdu," whereas for Césaire the desired object is spatialized as "pays." That it is lost, like Proust's time, is betrayed by the adjective "natal," with its implications of severance from an original plenitude. Even more important, however, is that "natal" is the clue signifier for a whole imaginary configuration in Césaire's work. For behind its signified, Martinique, lurks the illusory, original, unknown, phantasmagorical, and never-to-be-retrieved "pays natal" that is Mother Africa.

The grammatical subject is significantly absent from the title. If it were to be constituted in the title at all, its only logical form would be that of the possessive adjective, "mon retour." Yet this noninsertion of the subject in the title, its place taken instead by the indefinite article "un," coupled with the repetition indicated by "retour" opens a greater semantic space, which functions as a reflection of the often dizzying journeys of the self in this poem. In the title, the subject hovers somewhere between "cahier"—writing, language, and the Symbolic order—"retour"—some kind of repetitive representation—and "pays natal"—the lost, the absent, the Imaginary, the alienated. The implications of these Lacanian orders are far-reaching when we consider the spatialization of the geographical triangle that defines the subject, that is, France-Martinique-Africa, in the terms of the Oedipal triangle. France, that is, the French language, the Symbolic order, represents the paternal pole, and Africa, the Imaginary and desired, the maternal pole.

It is necessary, however, to avoid a reactionary reading of what Sartre calls Césaire's "écriture automatique engagée" when analyzing it within the parameters of the Oedipal conflict. We are dealing with a more complex poetic enterprise than one whose structures can be defined solely by the "anxiety of influence" and the need to rebel against the "Father" tongue. The violent alienation of the subject through language, the radical recuperation of that subject by an active transformation of that language and, by extension, its ideology—these are the struggles that structure the *Cahier*. The poetic dimensions of these struggles, ranging from the militant to the epic to the fantastic to the hallucinatory to the grotesque to the ironic to the self-deprecatory, cannot be reduced to single schematic articulations. Yet the Oedipal and geographical models of alienation, to the extent that they spring from and inform the *Cahier,* should not be forgotten.

Let us illustrate these considerations with a short passage from the *Cahier.* The image of the famished schoolchild punctuates the beginning of the poem as the first real human appearance in the text. Up until this point, the text has been zeroing in, in ever narrowing circles, like an airplane coming in for a landing, from "Les Antilles" to "cette ville" to "le morne"; from the geographical to the human, from the general to the particular. It now focuses on the child, innocent, offended, alienated, starving, victimized by racism:

> Et ni l'instituteur dans sa classe, ni le prêtre au catéchisme ne pourront tirer un mot de ce négrillon somnolent, malgré leur manière si énergique à tous deux de tambouriner son crâne tondu, car c'est dans les marais de la faim que s'est enlisée sa voix d'inanition (un mot-un-seul-mot et je-vous-en-tiens-quitte-de-la-reine-Blanche-de-Castille, un mot-un-seul-mot, voyez-vous-ce-petit-sauvage-qui-ne-sait-pas-un-seul-des-dix-commandements-de-Dieu).
> car sa voix s'oublie dans les marais de la faim,
> et il n'y a rien, rien à tirer vraiment de ce petit vaurien,
> qu'une faim qui ne sait plus grimper aux agrès de sa voix
> une faim lourde et veule,
> une faim ensevelie au plus profond de la Faim de ce morne famélique.
> (p. 39)

The child is not named as such, but, rather, seen through the eyes of the others, two representatives of the accomplice institutions of the ruling colonial superstructure: the Church and the school system. The boy is reified into racial stereotypes: "ce négrillon somnolent," "ce petit vaurien." Yet there is no mistaking the irony of this passage. The image of the teacher and the priest trying to extract an alienated response from the child is pitted against the more fundamental reality of his hunger. The absurdity lies in the discrepancy between their efforts and the objective reality to which they are blinded. Their discourse, initially espoused in the text by the poet's seeing the boy from their point of view, is transformed into parody, marked by its confinement within the boundaries of the parentheses, reduced to meaningless formulae by the dashes between the words. The violence of the discourse that they seek to impose is evident both in form, "leur manière si énergique à tous deux de tambouriner son crâne tondu," and in the bitter irrelevance of its content, "la reine Blanche de Castille." The reader cannot miss the final irony of the white queen, as far away in time, space, and race from Martinique as possible.

In defense of the child, Césaire blames hunger as the true enemy, signaling economic as well as cultural deprivation. The text supports the child against the others in the breakdown between prose and verse. The "scene" between the pupil and the figures of white authority is articulated in prose, whereas the hunger "qui ne sait plus grimper aux agrès de sa voix" becomes, unexpectedly, a source of poetry. This is an example of the subject's desired poetic praxis, as pronounced later in the *Cahier:* " 'Ma bouche sera la bouche des malheurs qui n'ont point de bouche' " (p. 61).

We can contrast this passive, speechless stance in the face of authority figures with two alternative poetic positions to which the subject has recourse. The first of these is a denouncing of the enemy through language, a devalorizing of the other's institutions by means of poetic reversals of values:

Parce que nous vous haïssons, vous et
votre raison, nous nous réclamons de la
démence précoce de la folie flamboyante
du cannibalisme tenace

Trésor, comptons:
la folie qui se souvient
la folie qui hurle
la folie qui voit
la folie qui se déchaîne

(p. 73)

Madness *qua* madness is not what is being exalted here. Nor is the simplistic, romanticized madness-is-truth of the Surrealists. Madness is valorized because of its oppositional function in relation to reason, but the text articulates still more of a structure and purpose for madness than being only nonreason. First, madness must remember, as a prerequisite to any consciousness raising, and it is contrasted in the text with the negative descriptions of "ces pays sans stèle, ces chemins sans mémoire, ces vents sans tablette" (p. 71). Memory is at the crossroads of ontology and epistemology in the *Cahier,* for the subject and for the people. Not to remember is a form of ignorance or misprision. The content of the memory is fixed, although its manifestations may vary: it is the memory of enslavement and exile. Second, madness screams. Unlike the child, or the people, "à côté de leur vrai cri," there is a double liberation implied here, in finding a voice and in exaggerating it beyond the limits of the acceptable. Third, madness sees, as opposed to another form of misprision, which is mystification. And, last, madness unleashes itself, playing on "chains," with its connotations of enslavement.

The second, related way of opposing the language of the other is by turning it around on itself, by making the poetic praxis into an arm, of *engagement,* of revolution, of cosmic change, by wreaking destruction with words:

> des mots, ah oui, des mots! mais
> des mots de sang frais, des mots qui sont
> des raz-de-marée et des érésipèles
> des paludismes et des laves et des feux
> de brousse, et des flambées de chair,
> et des flambées de villes . . .

> (p. 87)

This passage constitutes a revolutionary call to arms, in which the image, drawing upon the destructive forces in the cosmos, is called upon to renew itself and the world around it. But the image depends upon the writing subject for its articulation, and for the subject nothing is given, nothing can be taken for granted. No sooner is it constituted in language than it can be annihilated again, no sooner does it find a linguistic bridge that allows it to substitute itself for a larger community with which it desires to identify, than this fragile union breaks apart, condemning the subject to its solipsistic world. The subject of the *Cahier* is a history of these problems. The text poses these problems. We cannot hope to give a reading of the *Cahier* without confronting the problematized subject.

The subject comes into being in poetic discourse. It is our contention throughout this study that Césaire's use of poetry, with its self-imposed formal restrictions, is an experimentation with the concepts of delimitation, identification, definition, and freedom. Being, knowledge, and poetry are coextensive, mutually informing each other dialectically.

In certain poems, the subject comes into being within the boundaries of the text with a natural grace and simplicity reminiscent of fetal growth within the womb. In other texts, it is as if the subject imposed the tightest strictures of structure around itself only to see if, Houdini-like, it could break out of them into freedom. Since a poem is both language and space, an island of matter in a sea of space, the subject's use of this spatialization informs our reading throughout. The poetic frontiers can be open in innocence or in welcome, closed in fear or in defiance. The subject can expand the limits or narrow the parameters, be born into freedom or pushed out into exile.

These relationships are never static. Each poem is a new exploration for the subject. It starts from zero, as it were, forcing itself to find the way to constitute itself. The subject does not "know" outside of its text, and we cannot speak of a progress from the *Cahier* to the last poems of *Ferrements* or *Noria*. The later poems rework the *Cahier* and clarify its form, but they do not change the dialectics of the subject. They can be compared to the later paintings of Mark Rothko, where the parameters of the canvas are accepted as constant and are self-consciously articulated by the artist as the boundary within which an infinite play on finite possibilities is achieved.

But the *Cahier* offers the reader none of the neat borders of a short text. It is, on the contrary, the first articulation of the problem, and the subject is constantly finding itself and losing itself again, being decentered, writing itself, reading itself, and erasing itself. The text abounds in contradictory moments of selfhood for the subject that must be appropriated as the diagnostic tools for a diacritical reading of the relationship between *engagement* and a language of the self. To give a close reading of the entire *Cahier* is beyond the scope of this study and would constitute an entire study itself. Instead, we would like to trace a series of stagings of the poetic subject in what constitutes approximately the middle third of the poem. This reading begins on page 57 of the *Cahier* with the first intervention of the true grammatical subject. (It will often be necessary to quote at length from the *Cahier* in this discussion.)

> Au bout du petit matin, le vent de jadis qui s'élève, des fidélités trahies, du devoir incertain qui se dérobe et cet autre petit matin d'Europe . . .
>
> Partir.
>
> (p. 57)

The repetition of the refrain "au bout du petit matin," which has served until now in the poem as a haunting reminder of the inescapable rhythms of daily Martinican life in all its misery, takes on a different function when pitted against the otherness of "cet autre petit matin d'Europe." Suddenly, a whole spatial and temporal dimension is opened up in the text, *hic et nunc*, versus there and then. "Jadis" and "trahies" are the signals that we are about to embark on a textual history, a subjective remembering. "Europe" indicates a geographical jump, and the ellipsis opens up a suspension in time and space in the text, and of disbelief in the reader. What is of importance here is not the pinpointing of the exact locus where the *Cahier* is being written, that is, Martinique or Europe, or which experiences described are contemporaneous with the writing (this is an impossibility) but, rather, the interstices, the suspension, the undefined space across the ocean, the temporal possibilities of the infinitive and conditional verbs, the voyage and not the arrival, the process and not the product.

For the un-definition, if we may call it that, of the space between "Europe . . ." and "Partir" is that area in which the subject begins to constitute itself poetically, a mental area and a poetic space where creativity and identity interact. In contrast to Césaire's later poems where identity is linked to constraint, the *Cahier* produces a series of textual expanses and temporal transitions out of which the text creates numerous different subjects.

"Partir." Period. The marvelous succinctness of the single word and its punctuation are contradicted by its infinitive ending and the liberation implied in the meaning of "to leave." In a later poem entitled "C'est moi-même, Terreur, c'est moi-même," Césaire declares, citing Rimbaud, "on ne part pas, on ne part jamais." [2] But here, "partir" connotes a threshold as well as a voyage, a kind of on-the-verge-of, which sets in motion a whole tense-desiring mechanism for the subject:

Comme il y a des hommes-hyènes et des hommes-panthères, je serais un
    homme-juif
un homme-cafre
un homme-hindou-de-Calcutta
un homme-de-Harlem-qui-ne-vote-pas

L'homme-famine, l'homme-insulte, l'homme-torture . . .

(p. 57)

The conditional tense of the verb "to be" which identifies the subject is arresting and extraordinary, even in a poetic text. It is the condition/al of dis-alienation. It articulates the subject's desire and manages to hold it suspended in time, neither quite past nor entirely present, nor yet to come, and it indicates the presence of an intrasubjective dialogue. What follows is the magnitude of the wish for *engagement,* for identification. The common denominator of these global types is their shared status as the oppressed and the humiliated of the world. But the subject's desire to be one with them is deconstructed by the ways in which it represents them. The hyphenated descrip-

2. Césaire, "C'est moi-même, Terreur, c'est moi-même," *Ferrements* (Paris: Editions du Seuil, 1960), p. 29.

tions amount to a reification, a depersonalization, a reduction to types which degenerates further from the specific racial or geographical categories to more generalized abstractions of moral outrage. There is a certain "splendeur" to this "misère," a narcissistic aspect to this *engagement* which the subject qualified previously as "fidelités trahies" and which the text denounces with the violent question that follows this passage: "mais est-ce qu'on tue le Remords?"

As we have stated, identity and the poetic praxis are inextricably linked, and the *Cahier* is a history of both, and of the relationship between the two. This is evidenced by the contiguity of the two projects in the section of the *Cahier* under analysis here. For the poetic immediately follows the existential-engaged. And the grandiosity of the subject's poetic intention mirrors that of its wish to stand for all of oppressed humanity:

> Je retrouverais le secret des grandes communications et des grandes combustions. Je dirais orage. Je dirais fleuve. Je dirais tornade. Je dirais feuille. Je dirais arbre. Je serais mouillé de toutes les pluies, humecté de toutes les rosées. Je roulerais comme du sang frénétique sur le courant lent de l'œil des mots en chevaux fous en enfants frais en caillots en couvre-feu en vestiges de temple en pierres précieuses assez loin pour décourager les mineurs. Qui ne me comprendrait pas ne comprendrait pas davantage le rugissement du tigre.
>
> (p. 59)

There is a chiasmatic structure to this passage that is worthy of note since it addresses the questions of reading and writing. The subject's poetic quest at the beginning of the passage is for the hidden, the great, the bridges of language that constitute meaning. This is linked to the secrets of nature and by extension to the entire cosmos. The all-encompassing "toutes" function as semantic equivalents of "l'homme" in the previous passage, both being figures of generalization. As the subject was both magnified and lost by its identification with the faceless sea of humanity that it paradoxically rendered meaningless in the first passage, so in this next passage does the grandiose desire to be penetrated by and to speak of the whole cosmos in order to reveal the secrets of the "grandes communications" disintegrate into disembodied, detached, isolated words, fragments. But what is more problematic is this: in the first part of this passage, the poetic enterprise of the subject, however unrealistically, sought to represent, reveal, and unify language and cosmos, whereas the passage ends with a reversal of these values. And this is not a question of the general modulating to the particular, for the particular does not have value as synecdoche here. The words are particles, not even parts. The reader is deprived of discovering their meaning by the subject's solipsistic gesture that will hide it, burying it like "pierres précieuses assez loin pour décourager les mineurs." What the subject of the beginning discovers, the subject of the end dissimulates, defying the reader in the process.

The "I would be" and the "I would say" passages serve as mirror images of one another. Both articulate a loss for the subject compared with its original ambition. And their lesson is paradigmatic: the general, the abstract, the collective cannot be posited a priori if the subject is not yet defined and identified. Their nature is relational, not absolute. Poetic discourse produces a subject first, and then a means of knowledge for that subject. "A moi. L'histoire d'une de mes folies," says Rimbaud in "Alchimie du verbe." "A moi. L'histoire de ma lâcheté," says Césaire.

In this part of the *Cahier,* there is yet a third possible identification that the subject attempts, that of the poet with Christ:

> Partir. Mon coeur bruissait de générosités emphatiques. Partir . . . j'arriverais lisse et jeune dans ce pays mien et je dirais à ce pays dont le limon entre dans la composition de ma chair: "J'ai longtemps erré et je reviens vers la hideur désertée de vos plaies."
>
> Je viendrais à ce pays mien et je lui dirais: "Embrassez-moi sans crainte . . . Et si je ne sais que parler, c'est pour vous que je parlerai."
>
> Et je lui dirais encore:
>
> "Ma bouche sera la bouche des malheurs qui n'ont point de bouche, ma voix, la liberté de celles qui s'affaissent au cachot du désespoir."
>
> (p. 61)

The Christian vocabulary, the biblical tone, the prodigal son imagery, and the humble attitude of this passage are belied by the way in which they are presented. The imperfect tense that initiates the passage is a signal that the subject is already presenting it as history or text. The subject comments on itself here, demystifying its own Christian temptation. This is underlined by the ironic use of quotation marks in the text. By quoting itself as if it were already poetry or gospel, the subject reveals itself as having been confined by a kind of textual grandiosity. The Christian temptation is also an esthetic one. To represent the other can constitute a betrayal on the part of the subject, as the subject confesses its need to tell itself:

> "Et surtout mon corps aussi bien que mon âme, gardez-vous de vous croiser les bras en l'attitude stérile du spectateur, car la vie n'est pas un spectacle, car une mer de douleurs n'est pas un proscenium, car un homme qui crie n'est pas un ours qui danse . . ."
>
> (p. 63)

This warning administered by the subject to itself is so obvious that it functions as a gauge by which the self could measure to what extent it is, really, on the other side of the "mer de douleurs," divided from its self, looking upon the distance it must travel to selfhood as if through the eyes of another. The apparent moral stance of this passage is, in effect, concealing a deeper alienation on the part of the subject, which fears the shock of reality.

But the *Cahier* is, as we have stated, the story of at least two subjects, and at this point what we might call the retrospective subject intervenes to narrate the "truth" of reality:

> Et voici que je suis venu!
> De nouveau cette vie clopinante devant moi, non pas cette vie, cette mort, cette mort sans sens ni piété, cette mort où la grandeur piteusement échoue, l'éclatante petitesse de cette mort . . .
>
> (p. 63)

The text articulates the difference between, on the one hand, the subject's desire, the unfulfilled, conditional mood of its hopes, the grandiosity of the dream of collective unity, and, on the other, the pettiness of life-death. This confrontation with the objective reality that surrounds the subject renders all that went before a *tabula rasa*. The link to the others, "ma bouche sera la bouche des malheurs qui n'ont point de bouche," is revealed as a metonymy of the impossible as the subject retreats into the defeated stance of its solitude. It is forced to reject solidarity as a mystification, a state that it attempted to impose from the outside, through representation:

> et moi seul, brusque scène de ce petit matin
> où fait le beau l'apocalypse des monstres puis, chavirée, se tait
>
> (p. 63)

Solitude and silence force the text to begin again. This is articulated conflictually. The passage that follows is a dialogue between the subject and itself. The mathematical vocabulary of precise measurements and constrictions is opposed to the abstract notions of "vie," "création," "homme," and to the previous visions of grandeur of the subject. But the subject does not go gently into this dialectical contraction. Before relenting, it protests:

> —Encore une objection! une seule, mais de grâce une seule: je n'ai pas le droit de calculer la vie à mon empan fuligineux; de me réduire à ce petit rien ellipsoïdal qui tremble à quatre doigts au-dessus de la ligne, moi homme, d'ainsi bouleverser la création, que je me comprenne entre latitude et longitude!
>
> (p. 65)

The ambiguities of this passage reflect the subject's shifting fealties. It is resistant to definition and limitation, but not just any definition or limitation.

The reader cannot ignore the indirect reference to island and horizon and the connotation of personal and creative imprisonment that identification with this locus signals for the subject. The attitude of tension, anger, even disgust articulated by the subject in this passage points to an even deeper doubt concerning the subject's relation to the *engagement* it ostensibly desires. For the brief moment of this intrasubjective dialogue admits that *engagement* from the viewpoint of the inside is a kind of reduction.

Conceptualization of "islandness" as a negative limitation, as a reduction, has a doubly isolating effect on the self. At one and the same time, the subject cuts itself off from identification with the "wretched of the earth" and with those "at home":

> me voici divisé des oasis fraîches de la fraternité . . .
> cet horizon trop sûr tressaille comme un géôlier.

(p. 65)

Instead of producing a bridge that would link the self and the others, the particular and the general, the Antilles and the world, the subject has managed to wall itself off, to set itself apart from those very others with whom it desires to be united. Having thus created a prison for the subject, the text proposes a way for it to break out. The subject now turns inward in a movement of evaluation. It must take stock from within its prison to see what keys there might be to freedom. The judgment of limitation can be exchanged, poetically, for form. The subject becomes the surveyor of form, the assessor of tools, the poetic cataloguer of a different inventory:

> Ce qui est à moi, ces quelques milliers de mortiférés qui tournent en rond dans la calebasse d'une île et ce qui est à moi aussi, l'archipel arqué comme le désir inquiet de se nier, on dirait une anxiété maternelle pour protéger la ténuité plus délicate qui sépare l'une de l'autre Amérique; et ses flancs qui secrètent pour l'Europe la bonne liqueur d'un Gulf Stream, et l'un des deux versants d'incandescence entre quoi l'Equateur funambule vers l'Afrique. Et mon île non-clôture, sa claire audace debout à l'arrière de cette polynésie, devant elle, la Guadeloupe fendue en deux de sa raie dorsale et de même misère que nous, Haïti où la négritude se mit debout pour la première fois et dit qu'elle croyait à son humanité . . .

(pp. 65–67)

What the political or social conscience perceived as limitation, the poetic conscience has liberty to redefine as form. The dialectical movement of the text from expansion to contraction is the necessary condition of the subject's potential to synthesize a new position later in the text, that of subjective *engagement*. Alone and isolated, the subject reflects upon the form its isolation takes, and how it can be trans-formed. The above catalogue articulates the subject's desire to see from the inside out, as it were, with the eyes of the insider. This necessitates a linguistic substitution, an elimination of the narcissistic position that preceded, where the subject proclaimed what it would say or be, to be replaced with a humble yet proud enumeration of what is, of what the subject can call its own. This metaphorical property creates a new, proper subject. We draw attention to the poetic formula that initiates the catalogue and is repeated throughout—"ce qui est à moi"—because of the way it differs from the possible "j'ai." "Ce qui est" comes before the self, as if to signify that the subject was immaterial in its creation. This is a less powerful, less glamorous stance for the subject that desired, earlier in the poem, to be the measure of all things. It must be inferred that language, too, pre-existed the subject.

Paradoxically, however, the reformulation at work in "ce qui est à moi" opens up a world of beauty and strength as well as of suffering and ugliness. In this enumeration, the geographical resurfaces in the discourse with all the powerful concreteness of the Antilles erupting up out of the sea. But this assertion of materiality, like the stuff of language itself, derives its full value only as its versatile capacity for substitution is acknowledged. For example, if we look at the series of images that follow,

> . . . l'archipel arqué comme le désir inquiet de se nier, on dirait une anxiété maternelle pour protéger la ténuité plus délicate qui sépare l'une de l'autre Amérique . . .
>
> (p. 65)

a first reading reveals a tension apparently derived from a choice of vocabulary that expresses the frail position of the islands scattered between two giants. A closer reading, however, shows to what extent the tension is due to the fine line between the very possibility of figuration and its tricky threat to destroy itself. This passage is a poetic commentary on the elusive quality of the linguistic tools at the subject's disposal. The markers of figuration are clearly present: "comme" and "on dirait." The equivalence that follows each is symmetrical but opposite: "le désir inquiet de se nier," on the one hand, and "une anxiété maternelle pour protéger," on the other. It is within these parameters that the dialectical tensions between the image, the self, and its geographical projections are inscribed.

This textual coming to terms with the tenuousness of the poetic project through geographical imagery now functions as the source of a positive revalorization of that geography, what Henri Meschonnic would call a new "forme-sens." It permits the subject to extend beyond its own borders in ever widening circles which embrace progressively the twin, the model, the enemy, the origin.

The mention of Haiti, above, engenders a new section of the text which deals ostensibly with the hero of the Haitian independence movement, Toussaint Louverture. What is the meaning of this section for the subject? The historical model to be emulated, and with whom the poet identifies, also functions as a poetic paradigm, an investigation into the form of *engagement*. The choice of instance and locus is particularly significant for the discussion here. The text presents a picture of Toussaint already imprisoned in France. This configuration of confinement is, as we have seen, one of Césaire's obsessive metaphors. The passage begins with the anaphorical repetition of "ce qui est à moi," thereby establishing a textual identification between the poetic subject and the subject of the scene. The passage constitutes a poetic redress of grievances. By metaphorically springing Toussaint from prison through a linguistic substitution, the subject also liberates itself. Not surprisingly, the substitution is effected on the signifier "white," by ascribing to it negative values or signifieds contrary to what we expect in the Western languages where white always stands for good and pure and black for evil and contaminated. This white/black polarization is pervasive and alienating, but as a linguistic entity it is susceptible to reversal which reveals its arbitrariness.

Jean-Paul Sartre analyzes the value-laden quality of the white/black opposition in this passage from "Orphée noir":

> . . . les deux termes couplés "noir-blanc" . . . recouvrent à la fois la grande division cosmique "jour et nuit" et le conflit humain de l'indigène et du colon. Mais c'est un couple hiérarchisé: en le livrant au nègre, l'instituteur lui livre par surcroît cent habitudes de langage qui consacrent la priorité du blanc sur le noir. Le nègre apprendra à dire "blanc comme neige" pour signifier l'innocence, à parler de la noirceur d'un regard, d'une âme, d'un forfait. Dès qu'il ouvre la bouche, il s'accuse, à moins qu'il ne s'acharne à renverser la hiérarchie. Et s'il la renverse en français, il poétise déjà: imagine-t-on l'étrange saveur qu'auraient pour nous des locutions comme "la noirceur de l'innocence" ou "les ténèbres de la vertu"? (p. xxi)

Curiously, Sartre imagines only one side of the hierarchical reversal, that in which black is valorized as good. Similarly, he speaks only of the "strange" linguistic effect this would have, and not of its violent function of refusal and negation. Perhaps the corollary of the reversal, in which white must become the evil, strikes too close to home to be admitted. But this blindness on Sartre's part does not discredit his argument; it only serves to reinforce it. Césaire's text, on the other hand, actualizes the corollary by repeatedly using white in a negative context and finally equating it with death. So we have these images of Toussaint as an isolated, island-prisoner of black courage in white France:

> Ce qui est à moi aussi: une petite cellule dans le Jura,
> une petite cellule, la neige la double de barreaux blancs
> la neige est un geôlier blanc qui monte la garde devant une prison
> Ce qui est à moi
> c'est un homme seul emprisonné de blanc
> c'est un homme seul qui défie les cris blancs de la mort blanche
> (TOUSSAINT, TOUSSAINT LOUVERTURE)
> c'est un homme qui fascine l'épervier blanc de la mort blanche

(p. 69)

Toussaint is exemplary; the retrospective victory granted him by the text is one of immortality. It is not he that died but white death: "la mort expire dans une blanche mare de silence" (p. 71).

Yet the passage eulogizing Toussaint ends with an interrogation. If the subject finds strength in its identification with this first hero of negritude, it is also painfully aware that such a triumph is circumscribed: "la splendeur de ce sang n'éclatera-t-elle point?" (p. 71). The negative-future-interrogative form is a plea of uncertainty about the relationship between writing and action addressed to Rimbaud's imperative: "La Poésie ne rythmera plus l'action; elle sera *en avant.*" [3]

Césaire stands within a different historical tradition. As Albert Memmi points out in the *Portrait du colonisé,* one of the gravest crimes perpetrated by colonization is that of erasing the collective history of the colonized. Textually, the model of Toussaint engenders the kind of dialectical progress-regress so characteristic of this poem. What the subject gains through its identification with Toussaint cannot bridge the gap between past and present. The glorification of blood is recorded in invisible ink, and this momentary escape into the heroic mode must, in its turn, be denounced. The text accomplishes this again by juxtaposing the reality of the present, signaled by the repeated refrain: "Au bout du petit matin ces pays sans stèle, ces chemins sans mémoire, ces vents sans tablette" (p. 71).

The present—illiterate, aphasic—deconstructs the poetic attempt to represent the past. Toussaint is absent; he must be recalled precisely because he is not present in the collective memory. But this is impossible. The enlightening effect of Toussaint's image then is paradoxically to negate itself. The writing of the past has no meaning when confronted by a present that does not have access to it. For the subject, the temptation to transcend present reality by

---

3. Arthur Rimbaud, "La lettre du 15 mai 1871," *Oeuvres,* p. 346.

inventing a glorious history has been checked once more. This engenders another textual reversal. If the written text has revealed its impossibility to mediate, the subject will attempt to compensate for it by revalorizing the immediate presence of the spoken word. And since there is force in numbers, the subject multiplies itself into the collective voice:

> Qu'importe?
> Nous dirions. Chanterions. Hurlerions.
> Voix pleine, voix large, tu serais notre bien, notre point en avant.
> Des mots?
> Ah oui, des mots!
>
> (pp. 71–73)

This apparent primacy accorded to the logocentric is quickly decentered in favor of the signifier gone mad: "nous nous réclamons de la démence précoce de la folie flamboyante" (p. 73). This quotation has been discussed in terms of its oppositional value in relation to occidental reason. We reread it here in the context of the problematic of the subject. For this feigned but textually operative madness is the possibility of a different kind of liberation for the subject in the passages that follow. We might call them "l'alchimie du sujet," playing on Rimbaud's subtitle to "Délires, II." It is instructive here to expand on this intertextual reference by quoting from Rimbaud: "Aucun des sophismes de la folie,—la folie qu'on enferme,—n'a été oublié par moi: je pourrais les redire tous, je tiens le système." [4]

The irony implied by the textual capacity to repeat and systematize the "sophisms of madness" is the aegis under which the following reading of the African, confessional, and "shaman" passages (pp. 75–85 in the *Cahier*) operates.

The section is initiated by a question posed by the (understood) other concerning collective identity: "Qui et quels nous sommes? Admirable question!" The subject's apparent willingness to comply with the question intentionally misleads the other (here also the reader) into thinking we are going to get a "straight" answer. In fact, in the preceding context, consisting of the praise of folly and the alienated question of identity (because it initiated with the other and not the self), these combine to produce a subtle, complex, doubly alienated answer which accuses the other even as it seems to be deferring to the question.

The "African" answer to this question is no simple, animistic, identification of the subject, a "noble savage," with his natural surroundings. In each instance, the exotic and animistic images of the first clause are denounced by

4. Rimbaud, "Délires II 'Alchimie du verbe,'" ibid., p. 233.

the menacing violent images of the succeeding clause. The latter cancels out the former, thus rendering the "African" answer impossible:

A force de regarder les arbres je suis
devenu un arbre et mes longs pieds
d'arbre ont creusé dans le sol de larges
sacs à venin de hautes villes d'ossements
à force de penser au Congo
je suis devenu un Congo bruissant de
forêts et de fleuves
où le fouet claque comme un grand étendard
l'étendard du prophète
où l'eau fait
likouala-likouala
où l'éclair de la colère lance sa hache
verdâtre . . .

(p. 75)

The denunciation implicit in the structure of this answer is that the subject cannot really "go home again," even in imagination, because Africa has been violently alienated from it. Simplicity has been doomed forever by the deadly machinations of colonialism. The latter has erased the very possibility of the kind of African identification it liked to use to its own destructive ends.

The second response to the question of identity is presented as a confession of guilt, yet its function is to exculpate. This is not because the text succeeds in exorcising any real guilt. The scope of the crimes confessed, their nature, their geographical and historical distance from the subject are all ironic statements. The origin of this confession lies not with the subject but, again, with the other. The subject is confessing to what it has been accused of, not to that of which it is guilty. There are "true" confessional moments in the *Cahier* (the mode itself is always dubious), such as the pained and painful tramway scene where the subject judges itself guilty of identification with the aggressor rather than with the black victim. But here one cannot help but think of the victim of torture from whom only the parrotlike echo of the other's discourse is extracted, not the truth. The subject remains intact, even as it seems to be accusing itself:

je déclare mes crimes et qu'il n'y a rien à dire pour ma défense.
Dances. Idoles. Relaps. Moi aussi

J'ai assassiné Dieu de ma paresse de mes paroles de mes gestes de mes
    chansons obscènes

J'ai porté des plumes de perroquet des dépouilles de chat musqué
J'ai lassé la patience des missionnaires insulté les bienfaiteurs de l'humanité.

Défié Tyr. Défié Sidon.
Adoré le Zambèze.
L'étendue de ma perversité me confond!

(p. 77)

This passage is "un/original" in another sense, as well. The intertextual reference to Rimbaud's "Mauvais sang" is obvious, as Jonathan Ngaté shows in his article "'Mauvais sang' de Rimbaud et *Cahier d'un retour au pays natal* de Césaire: la poésie au service de la révolution." One has only to read these lines from Rimbaud's text to realize that it has a powerful presence for Césaire:

Je suis de race inférieure de toute éternité. . . . je suis de la race qui chantait dans le supplice; je ne comprends pas les lois; je n'ai pas le sens moral, je suis une brute; . . .
Oui, j'ai les yeux fermés à votre lumière. Je suis une bête, un nègre. . . . Vous êtes de faux nègres. . . . Cris, tambour, danse, danse, danse, danse.[5]

However, Ngaté concludes of Rimbaud that "sa sympathie pour les nègres n'a été qu'un 'jeu' d'intellectuel et que Rimbaud-Nègre n'a été rien d'autre qu'un masque" (p. 30). What seems more pertinent in the Rimbaud-Césaire comparison, however, is not what Rimbaud's real sympathies might have been but the metaphorical value that the "Nègre" had for him. In Rimbaud's text, the subject's identification with the Gauls, the pagans, the niggers, is a dramatization of his alienation, of his battle with damnation, of his noncoincidence with self. Because "je est un autre," it is the otherness in the "Nègre" which functions in "Mauvais sang."

For Césaire, the "Nègre" is not a metaphor for alienation. The cliché images of the nigger that emanate from the other are the cause for his alienation. His subject is not granted the same latitude of poetic choice as Rimbaud's, except at the price of inauthenticity. The trick, then, for Césaire, is to find the poetic mode that permits the subject to identify with the "Nègre" and yet at the same time deconstructs the alienating clichés that subtend it. This mode is irony. The subject is skillful at this kind of ambivalent auto-denunciation, at this ironic manipulation of the other's stereotyped images. In a passage similar to the one that was quoted, poetic hyperbole underscores the double message of public revelation versus private truth:

Et puisque j'ai juré de ne rien celer de notre histoire (moi qui n'admire rien tant que le mouton broutant son ombre d'après-midi), je veux avouer que nous fûmes

5. Rimbaud, "Mauvais sang," ibid., pp. 215–17.

de tout temps d'assez piètres laveurs de vaisselle, des cireurs de chaussures sans
envergure, mettons les choses au mieux, d'assez consciencieux sorciers et
le seul indiscutable record que nous ayons battu est celui d'endurance à la
chicotte . . .

(pp. 97–99)

The presence of these passages serves varying purposes for the subject.
According to the colonial dialectic outlined by Fanon, Memmi, and Sartre, it
is the white man who creates the nigger. By confronting this reality ironically,
the text does not erase that meaning. Rather, it creates a space where multiple
meanings can be deployed. By consenting to inhabit the negative poles of the
other's images, the subject can then use them oppositionally and explore the
positive poles of its blackness. We know what "Nègre" means for the other. It
is now the subject's turn to define what it means for the self.

This is the way in which we read the following "shaman" passages. In his
article entitled "A Reading of Aimé Césaire's *Return to My Native Land*,"
Emile Snyder has called it a "numéro." This puts into question the integrity of
the text. Since all of the *Cahier*'s representations of the subject may be called
"numéros" in the sense that the text is a series of imaginative substitutions
whereby the subject is both identified and subverted, it seems somewhat dangerous to single out this particularly African representation. The subject appears to espouse the threatening and savage functions attributed by whites to
the African magician. It is less a parody of the savage by the subject than a
parody of the other's image of the shaman. As stated, it is also one of the
passages that comes under the dubious aegis of madness, which heightens its
already ambiguous status.

Let us read the passage in an effort to clarify its functions for the subject:

> voum rooh oh
> voum rooh oh
> à charmer les serpents à conjurer
> les morts
>
> .   .   .   .
>
> voum rooh ho que mes cieux à moi
> s'ouvrent
>
> —moi sur une route, enfant, mâchant une racine de canne à sucre
> —traîné homme sur une route sanglante une corde au cou
> —debout au milieu d'un cirque immense, sur mon front noir une
>   courrone de daturas

(p. 79)

The magic transformations effected by the African chant do not have any
bearing on the outside natural order that is their ostensible object. What they

unleash are associations to past "identities" of the subject: a possible personal childhood memory of tropical poverty, a racial identification with the slave, a representation of suffering and martyrdom in the image of a black Christ. This contact with suffering in turn reinstates the chant. But it is already a different chant. It is no longer the prayer of a confident magician attempting to reshape the material in the surrounding world through words. The shaman is a figure for the poet, and the passage is an analogue of the poetic act: poetry is revelatory of the self. It is not action. But the subject maintains the valuable option of trying to depersonalize identity-as-suffering by imagining an escape. The subject might be subsumed by its fusion with another space, another time:

> voum rooh
> s'envoler
> plus haut que le frisson plus haut
> que les sorcières vers d'autres étoiles
>   exaltation féroce de forêts et
> de montagnes déracinées à l'heure
> où nul n'y pense
> les îles liées pour mille ans!
>
>   (p. 81)

To escape. To fly away. The infinitive is the tense of possibility. To turn the entire universe upside down, a desire implied in the phonetic reversals of "féroce/forêts," "îles/liées" and in the semantic reversals of "déracinées/liées," "îles/liées."

This form of escape is denounced as the magic words are called upon once again, this time to project an originary fiction for the subject. In the context of its struggle to constitute itself, the subject imagines a lost paradise comprised of the luxury of passively renouncing responsibility for its identity, of accepting its definition from the other—but not from the enemy. The other here is the subject's alter ego, woman. We will discuss the diacritical relationship between the subject as "je" and woman as "tu" in more detail in chapter 3. In the following passage, woman is designated in the third person and functions as the possibility for expansion and multiplication of the subject. She both describes and fuses with the self:

> voum rooh ho
> pour que revienne le temps de promission
> et l'oiseau qui savait mon nom
> et la femme qui avait mille noms
>
> .   .   .   .
>
> et ses pas mes climats
> et ses yeux mes saisons

et les jours sans nuisance
et les nuits sans offense
  et les étoiles de confidence
et le vent de connivence

(p. 81)

The rich rhymes accentuate the harmonious quality of the vision in which everything is accounted for. But no sooner pronounced than denounced. The ideal past, with its lulling rhythms and harmonies, is an illusion of the poet-magician. The subject's momentary temptation to lose itself in a passive identification with natural and feminine beauty is contrasted violently to the reality of the present, which intervenes as an aggression. The subject has been caught napping, as it were. In renouncing its usual vigilance, it has left itself open to attack:

Mais qui tourne ma voix? qui écorche
ma voix? Me fourrant dans la
gorge mille crocs de bambou. Mille
pieux d'oursin. C'est toi sale bout
de monde. Sale bout de petit matin.
C'est toi sale haine.

(pp. 81–83)

The indigenous images of bamboo and sea urchin indicate that the attack comes from within, that once again the subject is subverted by its own internal tensions. It repeats the same lesson in a myriad of forms: that there is no escaping an identity that demands confronting the requirements of *engagement*. At this midpoint in the poem comes the sobering question and the violent response that the subject was seeking to evade in spite of itself. In the form of a dialogue with itself, the subject discovers its *mot d'ordre:*

Qu'y puis-je?

Il faut bien commencer.

Commencer quoi?

La seule chose au monde qui vaille la
peine de commencer:
La Fin du monde parbleu.

(p. 83)

We have stated all along that the *Cahier,* and the subject it produces, is an investigation of the process of poetic delimitation. In the apparent paradox of "beginning the end" lies the kernel of the process. The end is not something that the subject can proclaim, achieve, or know. To play on words, it cannot end the end, it can only begin it. But by understanding what it must begin, the subject can see what it must end. The simultaneous thinking of these two moments gives a new thrust to the text. The means available to the subject cluster around the notion of beginning rather than racing blindly toward an ill-defined end. The subject is no longer dispersed by its different identities. And all the power of the process is concentrated, not surprisingly, in the force of the word. The image is restored to its full destructive, oppositional potential. And the by-product of this procurement of weapons is automatic collective ownership. The subject multiplies itself into a plural army and challenges the enemy:

En vain dans la tiédeur de votre gorge
mûrissez-vous vingt fois la même pauvre
consolation que nous sommes des
marmonneurs de mots

Des mots? quand nous manions des
quartiers de monde, quand nous épousons
des continents en délire, quand
nous forçons de fumantes portes,
des mots, ah oui, des mots! mais
des mots de sang frais, des mots qui sont
des raz-de-marée et des érésipèles
des paludismes et des laves et des feux
de brousse, et des flambées de chair,
et des flambées de villes . . .

.   .   .   .

Accommodez-vous de moi. Je ne m'accommode pas de vous!

(pp. 85–87)

The allied images that are called into battle are the forces in the cosmos and the naturally destructive forces of the island, transformed from ravaged to ravaging. This is one definition of disalienation. In the dialectic of the self and the other, the existing order is momentarily reversed by the text. The other is called upon to define itself in terms of a subject whose existence was initially only a function of the other's own. The subject has usurped the place of the other. This is what Fanon calls the dream and the condition of decolonization.

None of this is static in the text, however. The subject is always obliged to assert itself by means of the poetic process. Commenting on the image, it opposes what appears as an arbitrary gesture to what is actually its very possibility to constitute itself and its fight not to be alienated in the process.

The next stanza is structured so that one enters into the argument through the eyes of the other. By splitting itself off into its objectified form, the subject

achieves a vantage point as both observer and observed. As observer, it specu-
lates skeptically as to its poetic praxis and, as observed, it can respond:

> Parfois on me voit d'un grand geste du
> cerveau, happer un nuage trop rouge
> ou une caresse de pluie, ou un prélude du vent,
> ne vous tranquillisez pas outre mesure:

(p. 87)

The menacing tone of this last verse represents a shift in point of view which
warns against interpreting the imaginative faculty as purely esthetic or abstract. For the subject, it is a means of self-knowledge, a way of passing
through the looking glass:

> Je force la membrane vitelline qui me sépare de moi-même,
> Je force les grandes eaux qui me ceinturent de sang

(pp. 87–89)

In his important discursive text on poetry, "Poésie et connaissance,"
Césaire speaks of the power of the image in similar terms:[6]

> Les garde-fous sont là; loi d'identité, loi de la contradiction, principe du
> tiers-exclu.
>   Garde-fous précieux. Mais aussi singulières limitations. C'est par l'image,
> l'image révolutionnaire, l'image distante, l'image qui bouleverse toutes les lois
> de la pensée, que l'homme brise enfin la barrière. (p. 122)

The image, then, is a means of connecting to the self, of finding the self. It
pushes against the limits of alienation, to reunite "je" and "moi-même." In
the terms used here, the poetic image is a means of self-fertilization and self-
birth, of producing and retaining the product. If actual birth is paradise lost,
then perhaps poetic birth is paradise regained? The notion of paradise evokes
its opposite, hell. Disalienation can be substituted for alienation only by passing through it and coming out on the other side, like Dante. Hell is the past.
But there is no freedom, either subjective or collective, without memory,
without history. And although the subject valorizes its newly won selfhood by
declaring the priority of its own desire, "je veux cet égoisme beau," the text
deconstructs this arbitrary proclamation by reinstating the regime of death.
The blood that nourished life is now associated in the text with the bloodshed

---

6. Césaire, "Poésie et connaissance," in *Aimé Césaire, l'homme et l'œuvre*, by
Lilyan Kesteloot and Barthélmy Kotchy (Paris: Présence Africaine, 1973).

of death. However, these are not only opposing forces. For the biological or-
ganisms, they are part of the same process. For the subject, death is present in
life as its past and its future, as Dylan Thomas says in "Before I knocked":

> Before I knocked and flesh let enter
> with liquid hands tapped on the womb,
> I who was shapeless as the water
> That shaped the Jordan near my home
> Was brother to Mnetha's daughter
> And sister to the fathering worm.
>
> .   .   .   .
>
> My throat knew thirst before the structure
> Of skin and vein around the well
> Where words and water make a mixture
> Unfailing till the blood runs foul;
> My heart knew love, my belly hunger;
> I smelt the maggot in my stool.[7]

But in the section of the *Cahier* under discussion here, the memory of
death is represented as yet another prison. Because it cannot be denied it must
be identified with, and because its forms are ignoble it threatens the subject's
self-esteem. The force that seems capable of sucking the subject back down
into the primeval muck is not an external one, however. It is narcissism's constant companion, self-hatred, and when the two clash they provoke the subject's ambivalent desire for escape:

> Ma mémoire est entourée de sang. Ma mémoire a sa ceinture de cadavres! . . .
> nos révoltes ignobles, pâmoisons d'yeux doux d'avoir lampé la liberté
>   féroce . . .
> Ma dignité se vautre dans les dégobillements . . .
>   pour un bond par-delà la nage verdâtre et douce des eaux de l'abjec-
>   tion! . . .
> et il n'y a que les fientes accumulées de nos mensonges—et qui ne répon-
>   dent pas.
>
> (pp. 91–93)

Once again, there is no escape. Or, rather, the fantasy of escape is itself
one of the lies, perhaps the worst of them all, since it reveals the subject at its
most cowardly and therefore most worthy of self-hatred. The obscenity that
qualifies the lies is the most extreme aspersion that the subject can cast both
on itself and on the poetry that allowed it to be so constituted. But to wallow

7. Dylan Thomas, *Collected Poems*, p. 8.

in its own poetic dung does not even provide the subject with the perverted gratification of self-pity. For the lies disintegrate into silence. The text must take a different tack altogether.

This approach comes in the form of a narrative related allegorically to what preceded it in the text. It is a description of horse sales in Martinique, which ends with a scathing indictment of false appearances. The trading takes place on "De PROFUNDIS Street": "Et c'est de la Mort véritablement, de ses mille mesquines formes locales . . . que surgit vers la grande-vie déclose l'étonnante cavalerie de rosses impétueuses" (p. 95). The false picture of life and health that the dealers attempt to portray by substituting wasp bites and water for "rotondités authentiques" is analogous to the same truth and error, authenticity and grandiosity, that motivate the subject's quest. It has a demystifying effect as well, since it deconstructs Césaire's privileged identification with the horse, usually a figure for unbridled natural strength, freedom, energy, life, and the certainty of a poetic symbol. Furthermore, as a metaphor for the slave trade, it warns against any temptation to romanticize the latter. The lesson that this narrative contains for the subject is obvious when the self associates these misleading appearances with its own false stances:

> Je refuse de me donner mes boursouflures comme d'authentiques gloires.
> Et je ris de mes anciennes imaginations puériles.
>
> (p. 97)

The very concept of authentic glories is erroneous in a context of deception and horror and forces the subject to admit that it has mis-read the past. Mis-reading necessarily entails mis-writing, and in an effort to strip the text, its self, and history of all illusion and error, the subject proceeds to commit an equivalent crime in the opposite direction. The confessions that follow, in their utter self-derision that borders on irony, bear the mark of an effort to erase what went before. Yet the real effect of these cleansing revelations is to remotivate the dialectical structure that subtends the text.

First, the subject presents us with a new reading of the collective past which is meant to demystify all who would glorify it. This reading is problematic because, on the one hand, it is projected in a moment of deep disillusionment with self and, on the other, because the subject seems to imply that a certain historical truth must be denied in order to eliminate reactionary nostalgia for it:

> Non, nous n'avons jamais été amazones du roi du Dahomey, ni princes de Ghana avec huit cents chameaux, ni docteurs à Tombouctou Askia le Grand étant roi, ni architectes de Djénné, ni Madhis, ni guerriers.
>
> (p. 97)

Is the subject really so blinded by its own self-disgust? The text tells us something different. The willed denial of the past is belied by the precise details with which it is represented. The underlying truth that justifies the suppression of the past is its discontinuity, its inability to inform the present in any unifying, constructive way. The message is really for the other, who has alienated the subject, both individual and collective, from its history by pretending to deny it and by substituting for it the more immediate, undeniable past of slavery. As the subject pretends that part of its history may be denied, so it pretends to accept that part of its history must be accepted passively, that, indeed, the original acceptance of the horror of slavery condemns the subject to passivity:

> J'entends de la cale monter les malédictions enchaînées, les hoquettements des mourants, le bruit d'un qu'on jette à la mer . . . les abois d'une femme en gésine . . . des raclements d'ongles cherchant des gorges . . . des ricanements de fouet . . . des farfouillis de vermine parmis les lassitudes. . . .
>
> (pp. 99–101)

Is there no other option than to repeat the past? Is it possible that within the form of the repetition may lie the seeds of protest and change? Not yet, in any event. The subject presents this darkest hour of the slave past with which it is identified in order to explore the alternative reactions to it. In an effort to integrate past horror into present reality, to read the past as a way of understanding the present, the self first gives in to that "lassitude." Like the Holocaust, the suffering and degradation of enslavement are so unbearable as to provoke an identification with the aggressor. This confuses the issues of cause and effect, master and slave. That the subject momentarily passes over to the other side is borne out in the text by the passage from first to third person:

> Rien ne put nous insurger jamais vers quelque noble aventure désespérée.
> Ainsi soit-il, ainsi soit-il.
> Je ne suis d'aucune nationalité prévue par les chancelleries
> Je défie le craniomètre. Homo sum etc.
> Et qu'ils servent et trahissent et meurent
> Ainsi soit-il. Ainsi soit-il. C'était écrit dans la forme de leur bassin.
>
> (p. 101)

The subject appears to allow itself to be read by a predetermined text that it had no part in writing and whose interpretation justifies its alienation and oppression. Yet its monstrosity is only a function of the other's limited criteria. This is implied by the diacritical function of two other texts which are at stake here. First, the formula of the liturgy is invoked to support the argument for confinement and resignation. But it must be read as sarcastic when juxtaposed to a second text that is hidden here. This latter offers a model that could transcend the limitations of an identity that can be defined only by the other's measurements, that is, "nationalité prévue par les chancelleries," or "craniomètre," found wanting, and therefore justifying its enslavement. This other text is Terence's "Homo sum; humani nihil a me alienum puto." [8]

That the text is only partially quoted, the derisive "etc." being substituted for the latter half, makes its status problematical but does not erase it. Is the subject mocking the futility of this humanistic credo in the face of narrowmindedness by only half-quoting it? Or does having recourse to it, in the Latin, with its inevitable connotations of culture, provide the subject with the possibility of jumping over that narrow-mindedness to reclaim its place in the family of man? Whichever way one reads it, there remains the problem of its being only partially present. Perhaps if the subject could quote it in its entirety, the passage that surrounds it would already have been refuted. The subject would no longer be trapped in the oppressor's dialectic but would already have achieved a liberating identity in the form of human solidarity. As long as it remains alienated from itself, it is condemned to be alienated from humanity and therefore cannot complete the quotation "Humani nihil a me alienum puto."

The subject must continue to force the limits of definition in its quest for the ever illusive authenticity that it claims to desire. Its alienation from self must find the articulation of the most extreme or critical instance. By critical, we mean here that which stems from a self-conscious state of crisis and that which seeks demystification by self-reflection. For it cannot be ignored that the often discussed scene of the Negro in the tramway is initiated by what Paul de Man calls "the rhetoric of crisis" and that we should therefore be sensitized to a possible blind spot in the text.[9]

The passage begins with a statement of apparent confession.[10] The subject tells us to read what will follow as an example (in the etymological sense) of cowardice:

Et moi, et moi,
moi qui chantais le poing dur
Il faut savoir jusqu'où je poussai la lâcheté.

(p. 101)

But the critical element lies in the problematic structure of "il faut savoir" which articulates urgency, on the one hand, and an impossible lack, on the

8. Terence, *L'Héautontimorouménos* 1. 1. 25.
9. Paul de Man, "Criticism and Crisis," in *Blindness and Insight*, p. 16.
10. See Appendix for the full text of this passage.

other. The latter discrepancy engenders a poetic tour de force of description, as if the subject were indeed pushing its cowardice in order to make it adequate to itself.

The hyperbolized images produce a specific individual who is, at the same time, what might be called "Everynigger." He is not so named in the text, but the allegorical mode is suggested by the capitalization of "Misère," personified as the creator of this horror:

> Et le mégissier était la Misère. . . . Ou plutôt, c'était un ouvrier infatigable, la Misère, travaillant à quelque cartouche hideux.

(p. 103)

What is also implied here is an analogy to writing. Poetry can easily be substituted for "La Misère." Is this horrible image of the Nigger, then, the end product of a means of distortion which can be attributed to poetic discourse? Is this abuse of poetry what, for the subject, "il faut savoir"? What is the meaning of re-presenting or reproducing the scene? On one level, of course, it is a pre-text for the subject's confession.

> Il était COMIQUE ET LAID
> COMIQUE ET LAID pour sûr.
> J'arborai un grand sourire complice . . .
> Ma lâcheté retrouvée!

(p. 105)

The subject's alleged crime is one of attitude. It has seen through the eyes of the others, the presumably white women in the car who were laughing at the Negro. It has succumbed, allegedly, to the ultimate alienation of trying to be the other. Yet the confession itself cannot represent a source of redemption for the subject. Paradoxically, it is the recuperation of cowardice, "ma lâcheté retrouvée," that is disalienating, but the subject is blind to this, although the text is not. The recuperative moment lies between the first articulation of "lâcheté" in the scene on page 101 and the "lâcheté retrouvée" on page 105 of the *Cahier,* that is, in the representation of the Negro. For despite the judgment on the part of the subject that he was "COMIQUE ET LAID pour sûr," it is not sure at all. What the text produces is unquestionably a figure that is pathetic, in the original sense of the word. The cowardice, then, would lie in the subject's refusal to accept the pathos of its own text and to recognize itself not only in the image of the Negro himself but also in the pathetic uncertainty of the structure of "il faut savoir." The referent for the cowardice is not the Negro, then. But it continues to function and points to the impossibility of unmediated knowledge as it undergoes the kind of dialectical transformation

56   *Engagement*

that we now recognize as the structuring element of the *Cahier*. The cowardice becomes "critical" in the sense of pivotal, as the a priori condition of the subject's humble identification with all that it has hated in itself.

Through poetic alchemy, the confused mixture of cowardice and blackness offers the subject a muddy mirror in which to see itself. The horrors around it, instead of functioning as the obstacle to self-realization, now serve as the means of self-reflection:

> Cette ville est à ma taille.
> Et mon âme est couchée. Comme cette ville dans la crasse et dans la boue
> couchée.
> Cette ville, ma face de boue.
>
> (p. 105)
>
> Je me cachais derrière une vanité stupide
> le destin m'appelait j'étais caché derrière
> et voici l'homme par terre, sa très fragile défense dispersée
> ses maximes sacrées foulées aux pieds, ses déclamations pédantesques rendant
> du vent par chaque blessure.
> voici l'homme par terre
> et son âme est comme nue
> et le destin triomphe qui contemple se muer en l'ancestral bourbier cette âme
> qui le défiait.
>
> (pp. 107–9)

The "boue" at the end of the first stanza above, associated with the degradation of the present reality that surrounds the subject, must be wallowed in, so to speak, in order to get back to the "ancestral bourbier." The latter is that unformed, undefined, primordial sludge from which new life will spring. This act necessitates a regression to the pre-individualized state, but it is compensated for by a generalization of the subject from first person to third. This articulates an expansive movement from within the confines of isolating narcissism outward to a collective identification. Concomitantly, the subject is released from shame through the vocabulary of exposure as conscience yields itself up to the greater force of destiny.

"Voici l'homme" is repeated twice in this stanza, echoing the Christian "ecce homo." The reference is not arbitrary, since the associations of humiliation, sacrifice and redemption, death and rebirth, that cluster around the Christian paradigm are present throughout the next stanzas of the *Cahier*, until the revelation of the definition of negritude, on page 117, where this reading of the *Cahier* will end. However, the comparison must not be exaggerated. Although the Christian exemplum informs the text here, and may even legitimize the subject's sacrifice, the inspiration and the telos are quite different.

The posture of truth, "voici l'homme par terre/et son âme est comme nue," requires a violent denunciation, a recanting. For the subject to become "l'homme," it must become its own reader as well, renounce its beliefs, disclaim its own text. This recanting is tantamount to a dissolution of the subject, "sa très fragile défense dispersée." Yet this very dissolution of the subject, and with it the ideological superstructures and secondary process thought by which it was constituted ("maximes sacrées" and "déclarations pédantesques"), is the very condition of its recovering its primary, primal self. The primal is both historical-collective and psychoanalytical-personal, and it is released and recuperated by the text's revalorization of nature over culture, of desire over sublimation and repression, of the maternal over the paternal, of the imaginary over the symbolic.

It is not surprising, then, that the text has recourse to surrealist imagery at this point. More important, woman, and, with her, sexuality and fertility, intervenes here. These instances alternate in the poem with a repeated catalogue of the people's supposed nonaccomplishment and permit a deconstructive reading of the latter. This catalogue is repeated three times, each time with a difference in accent so that what was initially a negative value judgment evolves into the very condition of value. The subject's relationship to this reevaluation is dialectical, and the synthesis that it achieves, as we shall demonstrate, is the concept of negritude.

It will be necessary to quote at length from the text here in order to point up the deconstructive value of the alternating passages and its function for the subject. This is the first catalogue:

> Ceux qui n'ont inventé ni la poudre ni la boussole
> ceux qui n'ont jamais su dompter la vapeur ni l'électricité
> ceux qui n'ont exploré ni les mers ni le ciel
> mais ils savent en ses moindres recoins le pays de souffrance
> ceux qui n'ont connu de voyages que de déracinements
> ceux qui se sont assoupis aux agenouillements
> ceux qu'on domestiqua et christianisa
> ceux qu'on inocula d'abâtardissement

> (p. 111)

The structure of this catalogue itself is important in terms of the revalorization that is being discussed here. For it separates into two symmetrical parts, divided by the conjunction "mais" which signals a contradiction. The negative form of the first part appears as an indictment in terms of technological values. But the second part of the passage demystifies this evaluation, negates the negative by positing, in the ironic assertive form, the alienating, abusive consequences of these technological achievements. The "ceux qui" are pawns, even grammatically, in this situation. This has a liberating effect on the subject, which initiated the catalogue in a moment of seeming resignation. If the people are not only not the active initiators of advancement but, worse, its victims, then they are endowed with the potential virtue of opposition, with the power to reverse that hierarchy by substituting their own values. This realization bursts forth in the text for the subject with all the force of revelation: "Mais quel étrange orgueil tout soudain m'illumine?" (p. 111).[11]

The interrogative form, the strangeness, the suddenness, and the unexpected transformation of shame into pride underscore the surprising element involved for the subject in realizing what powers it can command textually. The self-assured tone with which it now calls upon nature is the result of the preceding demystification of the technological. As long as the subject included itself in the other's oppressive, negative definition of the people as primitive, it was barred from recourse to the liberating power of the primal. Now, in that subjunctive that is really an imperative, the subject ushers in the reign of the surreal and the cosmic. The reign is destructive and regenerative, it breaks down barriers and engenders fusions; it is violent and gentle:

> vienne le bris de l'horizon
> vienne le cynocéphale
> vienne le lotus porteur du monde
> vienne de dauphins une insurrection perlière brisant la coquille de la mer
> vienne un plongeon d'îles
> vienne de la disparition des jours de chair morte dans la chaux vive des
>   rapaces
> viennent les ovaires de l'eau où le futur agite ses petites têtes
> viennent les loups qui pâturent dans les orifices sauvages du corps à l'heure où
>   à l'auberge écliptique se rencontrent ma lune et ton soleil
>
>   (p. 113)

These last images, quintessentially surrealistic, combine a dangerous and apocalyptic quality with a satisfying image of coupling. Desire is their common denominator. This first instance of the presence of the "tu" in the text, which we shall refer to as the intimate other to distinguish it from that other that is the enemy, is crucial. The extent to which the subject's very capacity to constitute itself in discourse is dependent upon the positing of this other will be the subject of chapter 3. But first it is necessary to examine the new thrust that the entrance of the "tu" gives to the subject of the poem.

The surrealist images uncover the "tu" as the object of desire. But the de-

---

11. Arnold, noting that this verse is a classical alexandrine, characterizes the revelation as "Racinian" (*Modernism and Negritude*, p. 161).

sire for the woman is a metonymy for a more vast desire which only begins with her. She is what allows the subject to conceive a new form for itself, and this through regression to the moment of the formation of the ego. Through desire, anal and oral elements as well as animal aggressivity have surfaced in the text:

> viennent les loups qui pâturent dans les orifices sauvages du corps . . .
> il y a sous la réserve de ma luette une bauge de sangliers
>
> (p. 113)

The latter image also binds language to desire and violence. But more important, the "tu" is present as a mirror for the subject, as the capacity for the subject to constitute itself reflectively, to be reborn in an infinite variety of imaginary forms without feeling threatened:

> il y a tes yeux qui sont sous la pierre grise du jour un conglomérat frémissant
>   de coccinelles
> il y a dans le regard du désordre cette hirondelle de menthe et de genêt qui
>   fond pour toujours renaître dans le raz-de-marée de ta lumière
> Calme et berce, ô ma parole l'enfant qui ne sait pas que la carte du printemps
>   est toujours à refaire
>
> (pp. 113–15)

The "toujours renaître" and "toujours à refaire," both in their form and in their semantic value, function in opposition to the verbal and semantic clusters in the catalogue: "ceux qui n'ont inventé . . . , jamais su dompter, exploré." The organic nature of the former is assimilated to creativity and even to poetic discourse. By seeing itself in the woman-mirror, the subject can assume its wholeness and its capacity for refragmentation simultaneously. The repetitive nature of the experience functions as the liberating reassurance that the subject will not be locked into either stasis or disorganization. This assurance permits a revalorization of poetic discourse and the subject's dissolution in it. The signifier is invoked as a gentle, maternal force, capable of conceiving and conceptualizing what the subject-child cannot, that is, the radically different realities of space and time in a single image, "la carte du printemps," susceptible to repeated reformulation.

Under the aegis of this new space/time, the text articulates a future of hope and rebirth which strengthen the fatigued subject. And as the word brought forth a new subject, so now this mature subject will, in its turn, be the source of a new "forme-sens," as Henry Meschonnic would call it. The form is first imagined in its sexual origins:

et toi veuille astre de ton lumineux fondement tirer lémurien du sperme
   insondable de l'homme la forme non osée
que le ventre tremblant de la femme porte tel un minerai!

(p. 115)

This fusion is recapitulated in the next stanza in the image of the "silo"
which is androgynous, being both phallus and womb, and from which will
spring the feminine form of the signifier, "la négritude," with its phallic characteristics. But the birth of this new form proceeds first from differentiation
and negation, as the catalogue is repeated:

ô lumière amicale
ô fraîche source de la lumière
ceux qui n'ont inventé ni la poudre ni la boussole
ceux qui n'ont jamais su dompter la vapeur ni l'électricité
ceux qui n'ont exploré ni les mers ni le ciel mais ceux sans qui la terre ne
   serait pas la terre . . .
silo où se préserve et mûrit ce que la terre a de plus terre

(pp. 115–17)

It is significant that "ceux qui" cannot be defined except to say that they are
the possibility for definition, that without them there is the absence of meaning, and, at the same time, that they are the superlative degree of meaning, the
quintessence of meaning. The centrality of their position is becoming secured.
   In this space is articulated "la forme non osée," which confers a degree of
collective authenticity on what might otherwise be a highly subjective definition. Like the catalogue, mirroring it in fact, the definition proceeds first by
negation:

ma négritude n'est pas une pierre, sa surdité ruée contre la clameur du jour
ma négritude n'est pas une taie d'eau morte sur l'œil mort de la terre
ma négritude n'est ni une tour ni une cathédrale

(p. 117)

The subject seems to have repeated the catalogue of nonaccomplishment as if
instinctively aware that the repetition would yield a meaning against which it
could define itself. It finds that definition whereby it can realize its desire to
identify with something greater than itself, "ceux qui," without falling prey to
self-hatred anymore. Negritude is imaged as a life-force which penetrates the
universe as opposed to exploiting it, as a process as opposed to a product, as a
revitalization and not a resignation, as a means of liberation:

elle plonge dans la chair rouge du sol
elle plonge dans la chair ardente du ciel
elle troue l'accablement opaque de sa droite patience.

(p. 117)

The choice of what negritude is delineated against is not arbitrary. For those who invented, explored, conquered are implied in the images of tower and cathedral, structure and construct, sublimation and repression. To these the subject opposes its negritude as an overtly phallic force. The image of negritude as phallus serves several functions for the subject. As a corrective device, it revalorizes the black man, symbolically castrated throughout the text by the forces of oppression. It is the perfect metaphor for the desired union between the subject and the primal forces in nature. It is the bridge leading backward to the primitive past and forward to a disalienated future, a bridge whose way is barred to those encumbered by the weight of "civilization." Negritude is Césaire's own neologism, and this is its first intervention in his poetry. The extent to which it functions as a bridge to the people is attested to by the fact that the signifier creates a new signified, that after the publication of the *Cahier* there is a "negritude movement," there are "negritude poets," and so on. Part of the positive function of this new definition is to permit a rereading of the catalogue, this time as a celebration of that which was initially perceived as lack:

Eia pour ceux qui n'ont jamais rien inventé
pour ceux qui n'ont jamais rien exploré
pour ceux qui n'ont jamais rien dompté

mais ils s'abandonnent, saisis, à l'essence de toute chose
ignorants des surfaces mais saisis par le mouvement de toute chose
insoucieux de dompter, mais jouant le jeu du monde . . .

Eia parfait cercle du monde et close concordance.

(pp. 117–19)

This coming-to-the-term negritude represents the real turning point in the text for the constitution of the subject of the *Cahier,* which justifies terminating our reading of the poem here. Beyond this point, one can say that while the introjected image of the other continues to hover around the subject, it no longer has the power to decenter it. The subject's attitude toward its assumed destiny is henceforth unshakable, articulated in the repeated "j'accepte" which punctuates the entire last section of the *Cahier.*

However, one cannot help but ask how and why negritude functions as *the* constitutive metaphor of the subject. We have just seen that negritude bridges the individual and the collective, unites poet to people and to universe. Its function, then, is rhetorical as well as existential. It is the capacity for the very kind of substitutive relationships upon which poetic discourse is founded. It is the condition that allows the subject to constitute itself poetically yet without isolating it within the confines of a solipsistic discourse. The writing of the *Cahier* articulates the poetic subject that will be created anew in all the subsequent poetry. It also leads to Césaire's major article of discursive prose on poetry, "Poésie et connaissance."

I would like to conclude this chapter on the subject of the *Cahier* with a brief comparison to parts of the essay on poetry that would illuminate this reading. The essay does not explain the poem, since it inevitably falls prey to the problematic rhetorical relationship that obtains when a poet writes prose about his poetry, as Enrico Mario Santí demonstrates convincingly in his article "The Politics of Poetics." Rather, our purpose in discussing Césaire's essay is to evaluate how "poésie" led to "connaissance." [12]

In the context of our reading, one might say that the constitution of the subject in the *Cahier* is what permitted Césaire to become a poet, and a politically engaged poet. Yet the subject's "connaissance" as articulated in the essay points to an *engagement* of a different order from that implied by negritude. For in "Poésie et connaissance," the speaking subject places itself in that long line of what Rimbaud calls the "horribles travailleurs," along with Baudelaire, Rimbaud, Mallarmé, Lautréamont, Apollinaire, and Breton—all French and all white. Does this identification with the language of the Father threaten to deconstruct the entire oppositional enterprise of the subject of the *Cahier* that has been outlined here? I would like to propose that the subject's triumphant assumption of its phallic negritude represents a unique solution to the Oedipal problem whereby the poetic fathers are assimilated to the ancestral ones. This is accomplished through the articulation of the opposition "connaissance poétique/connaissance scientifique."

We have shown how the nonscientific was recuperated as a positive, poetic value in the "ceux qui" catalogues. This informs Césaire's following indictment of the scientific in the essay:

> En somme, la connaissance scientifique nombre, mesure, classe et tue. . . . Il faut ajouter qu'elle est pauvre et famélique. Pour l'acquérir, l'homme a tout sacrifié désirs, peurs, sentiments, complexes psychologiques.

12. In *Modernism and Negritude,* Arnold discusses Césaire's essay under the rubric "Aesthetic Primitivism" (pp. 54–58). But he postulates an extratextual Bergsonian link which would mediate for Césaire between Western logic and African temporality, whereas my argument here centers around the textual function of the term negritude as the subject's constitutive metaphor.

Pour acquérir cette connaissance impersonnelle qu'est la connaissance scientifique, l'homme s'est dépersonnalisé, s'est désindividualisé.[13]

It is interesting to note that the depersonalization of the colonized usually attributed to the colonial situation is envisioned here as the by-product of a more universal mechanism in which technological man is seen as the alienated victim of his own "advancement." Césaire's argument prefigures Herbert Marcuse's in *Eros and Civilization*.

But the most salient point in the structure of Césaire's discussion is that it takes a detour before opposing science to poetry. The detour takes us back in time to the originary fiction of the "savant primitif":

> L'erreur est de croire que la connaissance a attendu, pour naître, l'exercice méthodique de la pensée ou les scrupules de l'expérimentation. Même, je crois que l'homme n'a jamais été plus près de certaines vérités qu'aux jours premiers de l'espèce. Aux temps où l'homme découvrait avec émotion le premier soleil, la première pluie, le premier souffle, la première lune. . . .
>
> C'est dans cet état de crainte et d'amour, dans ce climat d'émotion et d'imagination que l'homme a fait ses premières découvertes, les plus fondamentales, les plus décisives. . . .
>
> C'est cette nostalgie de brumaire tiède qui du grand jour de la science rejeta l'homme aux forces nocturnes de la poésie.[14]

Nothing is more poetic than this myth of poetry as nostalgia for myth. The importance of positing the myth is immeasurable. For it allows a rereading of the modern poetic enterprise in light of that very reversal of the civilized/primitive opposition that the *Cahier* attempts to effect. This is evident even in the imagery of the prose passage. The white-day image qualifies science as opposed to the black-nocturnal image of poetry.

Césaire goes on to read the historical function of poetry in the France of 1850 as subversive. By stating the case in terms of an adversary relationship, the poetic tradition becomes recuperable from the standpoint of negritude: "La nation la plus prose, en ses membres les plus éminents . . . passa à l'ennemi. Je veux dire à l'armée à tête de mort de la liberté et de l'imagination."[15]

The empirical discourse of science is vanquished by the imaginative discourse of poetry whose weapons are "violence, aggressivité, instabilité." But its function is not only destructive. It must also be constitutive in order to qualify as a means of "connaissance." It produces a subject, manifestations of

13. Césaire, "Poésie et connaissance," pp. 112–13. See also Césaire, *Discours sur le colonialisme*.

14. "Poésie et connaissance," p. 113.

15. Ibid., p. 114.

an individual's unconscious, which can be read as a text, and a collective unconscious, also to be read as a text:

> Ce qui émerge, c'est le fond individuel. Les conflits intimes, les obsessions,
> les phobies, les fixations. Tous les chiffres du message personnel. . . .
> Ce qui émerge aussi, c'est le vieux fond ancestral. Images héréditaires que
> seule peut remettre à jour, aux fins de déchiffrement, l'atmosphère poétique.[16]

The essay actually describes in different terms, without the anguish, the
subject's adventure in the *Cahier*. It enlarges upon the adventure by making it
the adventure of all poetry, but this would not have been possible without the
Cahier's initial articulation of the subversive function of the bad subject.
What the *Cahier* teaches the essay is that the roots of all poetry can be traced
to a nostalgia for the impossible plenitude of the primitive that civilization has
repressed. Through the revelation of its own primitiveness, the poetic subject
transforms the nostalgic mode into the creative one, establishing negritude at
the forefront of the opposition. The battle begins with a new signifier, constituted from past values combined with rules from the language of the other.
White is compelled to marry black. The word itself stands as a figure for the
very forcing of the limits of possibility that characterizes the *Cahier*. At once
primitive and poetic, African and ur-French, it combines what it needs from
the ancestral past and from the poetic past to forge a new identity for the subject. The subject has found a model that can reconcile its poetic ambition, its
intellectual *engagement* vis-à-vis the other "horribles travailleurs" of poetry,
and its visceral *engagement* vis-à-vis the people. This was not an a priori
goal. It is discovered in the very writing of the *Cahier*.

16. Ibid., p. 123.

3. The Subject and the Intimate Other:
Woman as *Tu*

. . . là où les femmes rayonnent de langage. . . .

Aimé Césaire, "Prophétie"

WE HAVE SEEN from the discussion of the *Cahier* that the textual intervention of woman as "tu" can have major consequences for the subject's definition of itself. Woman is an essential figure in Césaire's poetry, and there are certain lyrical texts that could qualify as "love poems." But in speaking of woman here, we are not addressing an erotic, archetypal, or even potentially political figure. We are concerned, rather, with examining the signifier that represents her, the "tu" that appears in tandem with the speaking subject itself. The presence of the "tu" is often what makes it possible for the subject to delineate itself, to delimit itself in discourse. In reading Césaire we are justified in wondering if "je" is here, can "tu" be far behind? Within the context of the colonial dialectic of otherness, the "tu" represents a different kind of other, a double, an alter ego, literally, another self. This is why we choose to call it "the intimate other." This dual relationship, what Lacan calls the Imaginary, has its own characteristics and its own problems. If the "je" and the "tu" form a couple, this does not necessarily protect the subject from certain forms of alienation, as when Sartre states, "autrui me vole mon monde." The focal point of the readings in this chapter, however, is the constitutive role that the "tu" plays for the subject wherever their dialectical relationship is dramatized.

The major source of reflection that informs our analysis of this relationship is found in Benveniste's *Problèmes de linguistique générale,* in the section entitled "L'homme dans la langue." In Benveniste's discussion, one of the salient characteristics of the "je-tu" relationship is a linguistic complicity, what he calls a "corrélation de personnalité" (p. 231). This binds the first and second person together in discourse, since " 'tu' est nécessairement designé par 'je' et ne peut être pensé hors d'une situation posée à partir de 'je' " (p. 228). Moreover, since Benveniste defines subjectivity as a fact of discourse, it follows that the couple "je-tu" can exist only as actualized within each instance of discourse. Last, although the two form a unit because of their "corrélation de personnalité," and because their properties are reversible, they are not equal or symmetrical. A specific opposition obtains between the two. Self-

65

consciousness proceeds by contrast, by positing the "tu" as difference. The difference is that " 'ego' a toujours une position de transcendance à l'égard de 'tu'; néanmoins, aucun des deux termes ne se conçoit sans l'autre; ils sont complémentaires, mais selon une opposition 'intérieur/extérieur' " (p. 260).

Thus, the subject and the other must be defined by each other, dialectically, and always within discourse. The ramifications of this analysis for our problematic will be illustrated by the three readings that follow. Usually, in Césaire's poems, "je" and "tu" are the signifiers for man and woman. But as we shall see in another poem, "Hors des jours étrangers," the "people" can be the signified of the "tu." It is no less an intimate other, but it poses its own problems, which will be discussed in the appropriate chapter.

The unique nature of subjectivity that is founded in discourse requires that the subject must reestablish and restate itself anew each time it appropriates language for itself. In Césaire's quest for being, each poem becomes the difficult scene of a different formulation of subjectivity. Since identity necessitates an acknowledgment of difference, the "tu" to which many of the poems are addressed, and in function of which the subject is defined, will also be endowed with a specificity that varies with each poem. In the three texts that follow, one taken from each of Césaire's three major collections of poetry, the nature of the relationship between the "je-tu," and the textual space that it deploys, are so compelling as to preclude, momentarily, the larger issue of *engagement.* And yet the exploration of the "je" and the "tu" is not an anomaly in a static situation. It is a dialectical way station which is the condition of the subject's positing that other relation of otherness, the "je-vous," or the "nous-vous" of the colonial situation. It is therefore necessary to include such an examination here.

In the first poem, "Le Cristal automatique" (*Les Armes miraculeuses*), the positing of the "tu" functions as a dramatization of the communicational need that subtends human desire (p. 39).[1] Lacanian theory explains the close relationship that exists between desire and language. One always speaks to or for someone, to or for something. In the same way, desire is always desire for. Both are based on the notion of absence, of "manque."[2] In this sense, the dialectical dialogue between "je-tu" is the source of the poem itself. The subject modulates between projecting the desired object and striving toward recognition by her or fusion with her, on the one hand, and being thrown back from her toward a clearer self-definition, on the other.

1. Césaire, "Le Cristal automatique," in *Les Armes miraculeuses* (2d ed.; Paris: Editions Gallimard, 1970), p. 39. This poem and others of Césaire's texts that are discussed here and in the remainder of this study are reproduced in the Appendix.

2. Jacques Lacan, "Au-delà du principe de réalité," quoted in Xavière Gauthier, *Surréalisme et sexualité*, p. 320.

In the repeated initial "allo allo" of the poem, we immediately recognize the familiar verbal formula used in telephone conversation. It evokes certain associations: distance, absence, a desire to communicate, here versus there, a reaching out from one interlocutor to another. However, the form of this prose poem is problematic. It continues in one long, unpunctuated run-on sentence of sorts, a monologue in the guise of a dialogue, which has significance in terms of the nature of the "je-tu" relationship as it is mapped out in this poem. The other, the "tu," is posited rhetorically in the beginning of the poem in a peculiar way. The subject preempts the question that she will presumably ask by answering it first, "pas la peine de chercher, c'est moi." This ellipsis of the question foreshadows a later ellipsis in the poem. The absent question is central to the poem. It is the question of identity, "who is it?" The subject is compelled to disallow the articulation of the question and to answer it at the same time. The absent question sets in motion the whole chain of signifiers that characterize the "moi" versus the "toi." It also reveals a strangely self-referential aspect of what is nominally a desire for the other. The subject defines itself first, without looking or listening, as it were. And the only indication it gives us initially of the presence of the other is based on an absence. Moreover, we have only to look at the poem's disposition on the page to realize that it is defending against this absence, that it runs on in a desperate effort to make a block of words that huddle together, filling in all the gaps, never letting the "tu" get a word in edgewise. The only graphic chink in the fortress of black printed signifiers comes, not surprisingly, after the first "c'est toi," where we have an ellipsis, a blank, a zero, a "trou dans le discours." This is followed by "c'est toi, ô absente." In the poem "Séisme" (*Ferrements*), the poet asks, "Essayer des mots? Leur frottement pour conjurer l'informe. . . ?" (p. 10).

And yet the "tu," by her very absence, is what motivates the discourse. "Pour penser à toi j'ai déposé tous mes mots au monts-de-piété." This phrase is an oxymoron, since there is no thought without words. But one could read this as a desire on the part of the subject to revert to that prelinguistic moment, to a time of fusion, of reunification, of presence. We have further evidence for this point of view in the image of "le pain et l'alcool de tes seins," where the breasts are depicted as a source of nourishing delirium, where the desire to assimilate, to incorporate, is not only an erotic one but also one that implies a throwback to the mother-child symbiosis, to a time before linguistic codes and telephone wires, to a time before separation. Associated with the breast is "l'envers clair de la terre," there where "je voudrais être."

In fact, the entire poem is structured around the associative poles designated by "je" and "tu." The subject articulates a "tu" that is an inverted form of itself. "C'est moi" is associated with "nuit," "mort," "noyé," "pluie." "C'est toi," on the contrary, is related to "journée blonde," "l'envers clair de

la terre," "baigneuse," "l'accroissement du cristal," "l'aube," "le maguey
éblouissant." The effort to reconcile the two poles, his negative, hers positive,
passes through desire, imagination, and the future tense, which is the sign for
hope in Césaire: "je voudrais être," "dans ma tête," "quand viendra l'aube,
c'est toi qui poindras." Furthermore, the "moi" defines itself as "l'homme
des cavernes," that is, a hollow, a concavity, a darkness, in opposition to the
"toi" who, although or because absent, is imagined paradoxically as "pléni-
tude," convex breast, "accroissement du cristal," and is associated with the
concreteness of "les îles" and "la terre," as opposed to the "moi" that is
drowning.

We are left with what seems to be a contradictory reading of this text: the
"tu," desired for the illusion of projected plenitude, is conspicuously absent,
whereas the "moi" seems caught in its own sterile web, automatically repeating the formula "allo allo," which should imply communication but instead
seems to indicate absence of anything but its own echo. What there is, the
series of "il y a" in the poem, is undesirable. One might also extrapolate that
if the "tu" were present, and, with her, dawn and the future, the present, that
is, the subject and its night, would have to disappear and, with it, possibly the
text also. Perhaps this threat of disappearance explains the ambivalence of the
subject's desire for the "tu," invoking her yet underscoring her absence.

One might also look to the title of the poem for some clarification of this
ambiguity. The word "automatique" of the title never reappears in the body
of the text per se, but its self-referentiality illuminates the automotivation
pointed out. As for "le cristal," it is repeated as part of the first definition of
the "tu," in "l'accroissement du cristal, c'est toi." As noted, what actually
accumulates on the page is three dots, signifiers of nothing, of absence. Could
"cristal" then be a figure for *écriture?* Both contain a hidden *cri.* The association of the term *écriture automatique* with the title of this poem seems inevitable. The stream-of-consciousness form of the text, the unwonted associations of images within it, its placement in the collection *Les Armes
miraculeuses,* all attest to its relation to the surrealistic poetic praxis.

"L'accroissement du cristal" also approaches "la cristallisation" in the
Stendhalian sense of the term, being that phenomenon by which signs are read
through the distorting lens of desire until they crystallize around the desired
love object, thus giving her an imaginary form.[3] "Cristal" also connotes wire-
less, by synecdoche, the crystal being that substance used as a corrective to
regulate oscillatory current. Without concluding, then, we can at least suggest
that there is a connection between "l'accroissement du cristal," the accumula-
tion of the written words of the signifying chain that is the prose poem, and

3. Stendhal, *De l'Amour.*

the analogous spoken word with its desire for immediacy conveyed by the telephone metaphor. All of these seem to converge in the "toi," both written and oral in form. She is absent as a dialoguing interlocutor from the verbal conversation because the subject has chosen to exclude her. The subject, which is *hic et nunc* in the text, prefers to keep the "tu" there and future. For absence need not only be threatening; it can also be a substitutive possibility. The text takes over the conversation, and the subject can experience the liberating effect of imagining the other without losing itself.

The second poem, "Totem" (*Cadastre*), articulates a completely different aspect of the "je-tu" relationship.[4] It is a poem not of absence but of obstruction. At first reading the text reveals this strange contradiction: a blatant absence of subject pronouns amidst a preponderance of possessive adjectives. Further, the possessive adjectives designating the "tu" far outnumber those for the first person. Some preliminary questions already suggest themselves: what is the difference between, on the one hand, having and being, and, on the other, saying that the "tu," the more sharply delineated of the two persons, constitutes a whole by virtue of the sum of her parts?

The "moi" is roaming the page in search of a linguistic space in which to intervene in the poem as a true grammatical subject. It never, in fact, succeeds in constituting itself as such, although it travels widely, back and forth, "de loin en proche de proche en loin." For that matter, the "toi" does not ever attain real grammatical status as subject either. According to Benveniste, this is tantamount to nonexistence, and the anguished atmosphere of the poem resides in this struggle for existence.

Where, then, is the troubling element in the text, the constraining, oppressive force that prevents the subject from constituting itself? What is responsible for the web of anxiety that is woven into this text-ure such that a subject cannot affirm itself?" "détresse"-"trahison"-"destructrice"-"venin"-"naufrage"-"captive"-"abîme"-"piétinez"-"sanglots"-"silence."

The distorted, ambiguous syntax of the one real sentence with proper grammatical subject in the first part of the poem, and the doubt expressed by its verbal form (conditional, negative, interrogative), leads us to posit the question of the status of the titular "totem." If we read that sentence as "comment le totem buvant dans la gloire de ma poitrine un grand coup de vin rouge et de mouches ne bondirait-il pas d'étage en étage de détresse en héritage au sommet des buildings sa tiédeur de cheminée et de trahison?" certain tensions

4. Césaire, "Totem," *Cadastre*, trans. Emile Snyder and Sanford Upson, bilingual ed. (Paris: Editions du Seuil, 1961), pp. 29–30. See Appendix. See also Catherine Lowe, "Vers une lecture de 'Totem' d'Aimé Césaire." Her study of this text inspired my own, for which I am grateful.

become evident which help delimit the framework within which and against which the subject/text is attempting to articulate itself. In a reversal of the usual ethnological connotations, the "totem" somehow is defined by the "moi." Yet what the "moi" can offer is ambivalent: "un coup de vin rouge et de mouches"; what the "totem" derives is equally worrisome: "sa tiédeur de cheminée et de trahison." The chain by which this is transmitted, a cynical, mock-progression from concrete "étage" to emotional "détresse" to historical "héritage," and the uncertainty expressed by the verb, whose form contradicts the usual assertive connotation of "bondir," all add to the poem's anxious atmosphere. We are faced with a poetic crisis, a modulation between affirmation and negation, freedom and constraint, phallic thrust and frustration or, worse, castration. The "totem," that hereditary emblem that should guarantee the subject's ability to insert itself into a chain of being and meaning, functions here as a disarticulating force, an alienating, castrating, symbolic father.

The "tu" is looked to as a source of possible mediation, as a liberation from these inhibitions. But Benveniste's category of correlation should already warn us that the "tu" cannot have any more sure claim to existence than the "je." The "tu" is trapped into identification by simile, "comme." The best that can be effected through positing the other is to emphasize her potential in language, to somehow squeeze a different signified out of the signifier, to extract "distraction" from "destructrice," to distill "vin" from "venin," to salvage "rire" from the wreck of "naufrage," and so on. These images are, indeed, intensely beautiful. But it is mere poetic desire, willing its creation into existence, like Michelangelo's trying to free his slaves from the stone. Words are not action. A cruel self-mockery attests to the arbitrariness of this enterprise, underlying the poem from the first, as the text opens under the aegis of the "sistre des circoncis" (an ancient music hovering just short of castration), and the "soleil hors moeurs," that Césairian symbol par excellence of strength, here unintelligibly out of control. The subject doubts its very ability to assert itself. "Gloire" is first declared as self-value in "vin rouge," then reduced to the humiliation of self-hatred in "mouches." In this tenuous state the "moi" asks the woman as other to testify in some way to its existence, but she is, as we have seen, equally impotent. The subject cannot even see itself in her "regard," which remains captive behind closed eyelids. And the signifier, the potential for metaphor, the "comme" that attempted to constitute the "tu," proves to be a gratuitous, inhibiting god, which justifies the call to destruction toward the end of the poem: "chevaux du quadrige piétinez la savane de ma parole vaste ouverte."

By the last sentence, the spatial options for the subject to move in have been severely reduced—so much so that the other disappears completely: the "tu" is no longer designated in any way. The presence of the subject might conceivably be deduced from "sanglots" but quickly self-effaces, in an ending worthy of Beckett, into "silence" and "nuit." Is there perhaps a hidden Oedipal murder mystery in "Totem"?

Is "Totem" a figure carved out of the subject's desire to individuate from and identify with the "tu," simultaneously, in language? In the case of this poem, such desire is impotent to effect a unified, total image, either of the "je" or, and consequently, of the "tu." Language, the other available tool, functions as an ambiguous, double-edged sword here, which disarticulates "je" and "tu" even as they strain to constitute themselves. It leaves only features strewn across the page like so many word-corpses after a struggle. And yet this dismemberment forms the "totem," and the poem, a strikingly subjective "totem" to be sure. In this sense, the discourse projects a third element that is external to the "je" and the "tu," Benveniste's "non-personne, il," and whose menacing, paternal presence seems to detract from the resources that should ordinarily be available to the subject. The "totem" has appropriated the poem, and perhaps the subject, too, instead of the subject appropriating the "totem."

Not all of Césaire's poems that attempt to incorporate the intimate other end in the land of hushed defeat of "Totem," however. Different geographies provide a more fertile space in which the subject and the "tu" may insert themselves more successfully. Such is the case of the third poem that we will discuss in this chapter, "Intimité marine."[5] In this text, we are far from the paralysis experienced by the subject in "Totem." On the contrary, the "marine" of the title is indicative of the flowing movement that characterizes this poem and of the possibilities of reflection and exchange that allow the subject to constitute itself.

Significantly for our purposes, it is the "tu" that is addressed repeatedly in the first part of the poem. She is immediately endowed with the strength to be the grammatical subject of several sentences. Yet she does not speak in the first person: her presence as "tu" implies the "je" of the speaking subject that defines her as such. If we look closely at these definitions, we see that they proceed by negation: "tu n'es pas" rather than "tu es." This form is ambiguous. On the one hand, as a form of litotes, it implies the opposite: "you are not this," in the sense of "you cannot be reduced to merely this because you are actually limitless." On the other hand, it can be read thus: "you are not this—but I cannot say what or who you are." What "tu" is not is either a confining shelter ("toit" and there is an aural pun here, too, "toi" which emphasizes a breaking down of the usual barriers of definition) or a suffocating death ("tombe"), but rather, by inference, a powerful force bursting out of

5. Césaire, "Intimité marine," *Ferrements,* p. 50. See Appendix.

and transcending limitation, as in the androgynous, container-contained "silo/ ventre" image. Neither is the "tu" static, having resolved all conflict ("une paix"). The sharp, alliterative "k" sounds and the interaction of assonances in "courroux," "couteaux," and "coraux" reaffirm the existence of an active, aware presence. A constant sense of potential force seems to hover around the "tu."

It is at this point that the "moi" enters the poem, although not yet as a defined subject pronoun. "Je" does not become the actual subject of the text until the second part of the poem. What is so important here is the "moi" in relation to the "toi." The "tu" is temporarily but lucidly qualified as none other than the projection and externalization of the desire of the "moi": "D'ailleurs en un certain sens, tu n'es pas autre que l'élan sauvage de mon sang" and, even more revealingly, "qu'il m'est donné de voir." It is what the subject sees of itself reflected in the other that gives it the force to constitute itself into a subject. The image coincides with what Fanon calls the muscular dream of the oppressed man in *Les Damnés de la terre*. And it is illuminated by Lacan's discussion of the infant's construction of sense of self by means of his mirror image, in the essay "Le stade du miroir."[6] For Lacan, however, it must be remembered that the resulting sense of self is Imaginary in the etymological sense, that is, based on image, "manque," not "realité," and therefore alienating. Such a reading would account for the threatening presences of "tombe," "funèbre," and "morsure" (read also "mort sure").

In spite of these potential menaces, the self becomes the subject in the second part of the poem with triumphant elation. The transition to this second moment in the text was made, as we have seen, through the mirror—"il m'est donné de voir," now transformed grammatically to "je me vois." In many ways, these two parts of the text are inverted mirror images of each other, reflecting and echoing one another and dependent upon each other for their existence. This relationship bears out Benveniste's reflections concerning the dialectical nature of the "je-tu" couple in language. "Je" could not be metamorphosed into the now active subject, realizing its own powers, had the potential in "tu" to be constructed into a subject not been previously conceded.

In fact, the first expressions that the "je" chooses to describe its newly found self, while appropriately phallic in terms of sexual imagery, are direct phonic quotations of the insistent, aggressive "k" sounds we found repeated in connection with the "tu." This links the "je" and the "tu," but it is also the first and last appearance of the "tu" in the second part of the poem. From here on, the subject breaks away and stands on its own, in a joyous declaration of

6. Jacques Lacan, "Le stade du miroir comme formateur de la fonction du Je," in *Ecrits I*, pp. 89–97.

animal strength. Many of the verbs here are reflexive, the acts self-referential, as in "je me vois," "je m'enroule," "je me déroule," "je me brise." This breaking away seems to render the other unnecessary. While sexually we might say that this represents a regression to an onanistic equivalent—and one cannot help but note the orgasmic rhythm of the sentence "Je frappe, je brise, toute porte je brise et hennissant, absolu, cervelle, justice, enfance je me brise"—on other levels this narcissistic acceptance of self signifies an optimistic assertion of self-discovery and independence. The "je" has found its "vrai cri" and is able to call upon all sorts of sources and resources now available to it, as if magically freed, for the first time. These include not only sheer animal force but categories of thought, morality, personal history: "absolu," "justice," "cervelle," "enfance." The "je" can play with signifiers because they have already been experimented on the "tu." Thus, "je ne tombe pas" derives from "tu n'es pas une tombe," and "je me brise" can be risked because "tu ignores tout silo dont tu n'éclates le ventre."

If the "tu," the intimate other, has been eclipsed, it is because she has fulfilled her function as imaginary alter ego permitting the subject to articulate itself.

As the subject is constituted anew in each poem, so is the couple "je-tu," and we have discussed only three ways out of many in which the relationship can be posed. It must be mentioned, although it should seem obvious, that the attraction of the "je-tu" couple is so powerful for Césaire because the nature of the binding has great metaphorical value as well. Thus, in the title poem of *Ferrements,* for instance, the chains that unite the subject and the intimate other are also linked to those of slavery:

tiens-moi bien fort aux épaules au reins esclaves . . .
.   .   .   .
où nous deux dans le flanc de la nuit gluante aujourd'hui
comme jadis
esclaves arrimés de coeurs lourds
tout de même ma chère tout de même nous cinglons
à peine un peu moins écoeurés aux tangages

(p. 7)

In this way, the linguistic enactment of the subject's relationship to the "tu" opens onto the possibility of pointing beyond itself and cannot be read in a static fashion. Even if the "tu," once posed, is transcended, she offers the subject the vital momentary illusion that its utterances have overcome fragmentation, and this permits the subject to continue its poetic explorations.

4. The Subject and Negritude

It is my intention here to examine two of Césaire's later poems that represent an articulation of the relationship between the subject and negritude and can therefore be read as rewritings of the *Cahier*. For if, as Keith Walker claims in his book, "d'oeuvre en oeuvre (soit poétique soit dramatique) il n'y a guère d'évolution à proprement parler au niveau des idées ou des images," we cannot draw the same conclusions concerning the progression of the self-imposed density of Césaire's poems.[1] On the contrary, we must question the constraints of structure and their textual function in the service of the subject.

The confrontation between self and negritude is a dynamic and dramatic one. Is it always conflictual? To what extent does this confrontation open onto possibilities of dialectical transcendence? For Césaire, the text is the locus of this drama, the possibility of the reenactment of various dispossessions of the subject in language. It is the means of defining the parameters of identity and self-control.

It is useful to quote here Freud's famous dictum of 1933 from "The New Introductory Lectures," "Where id was, there ego shall be."[2] The translation of this formula can be tampered with slightly, as is done by Lacan, for example, but the basic structure is what interests us. In its essence, it describes and prescribes the substitution of a future for a past as indicated by the verb tenses. It is utopian in this substitutive vision, for the verb implies work to be done. More important, it is the new, disalienated subject, the now-self-conscious I (ego), that will replace what for Freud was the victimized, traumatized id of the past. In psychoanalysis, this substitution is effected through discourse. The primacy given to language in the constitution of the subject is identical in poetry.

In "Corps perdu" we are struck by a subject that vacillates between polarities, trying on different identities.[3] The "corps" that is "perdu" is not the same throughout the text. There are many modes of losing one's self, one's body, and many modes of retrieving them. In other words, we might say that the corpus of the poem constitutes the subject's lost and found.

To expand outward from this position is an ever present concern for Cé-

1. Walker, *La Cohésion poétique de l'œuvre césairienne*, p. viii.
2. Sigmund Freud, "The New Introductory Lectures to Psycho-Analysis," in *The Standard Edition of the Complete Psychological Works,* 22:80.
3. Césaire, "Corps perdu," *Cadastre,* pp. 80–82. See Appendix.

saire. Defining identity means defining racial identity, and the coming to self-hood through poetry is coextensive, for Césaire, with the assuming of his negritude. As Sartre says in "Orphée noir":

> Le nègre, comme le travailleur blanc, est victime de la structure capitaliste de notre société. . . . Mais . . . puisqu'on l'opprime dans sa race et à cause d'elle, c'est d'abord de sa race qu'il lui faut prendre conscience. . . . Le nègre ne peut nier qu'il soit nègre . . . : il est noir. Ainsi est-il occulé à l'authenticité: insulté, asservi, il se redresse, il ramasse le mot de "nègre" qu'on lui a jeté comme une pierre, il se revendique comme noir, en face du blanc, dans la fiérté. (pp. xxiii–xiv)

Césaire's poetic struggle for freedom, simultaneously individual and collective, subjective and political, psychological and social, is riddled with pain, self-doubt, efforts at evasion, shame, self-hatred. But we believe that certain of the poems can be read as the articulation of a successful solution to this problematic, that these texts function as the actual scene of a personal and political liberation.

If we trace the subject's voyage through "Corps perdu" we see that it begins as far away from "home" as possible, literally halfway around the world in Indonesia, grandiosely identified with the globe, only to shrink to a tenser, closer, more personal internal space, and from there to self-confrontation.

In the beginning is the end. The island of Krakatoa, like Césaire's native Martinique, is a volcanic one whose volcano nearly destroyed it. The volcano is a privileged image for Césaire, since its eruption has both destructive and constructive powers. Out of its force comes the possibility of the islands. The spitting "k" sounds of "Krakatoa," especially as combined with "moi qui," make it wonderfully onomatopoetic as well.[4]

4. Arnold has performed a meticulous and impeccable phonological analysis on these first seven lines, demonstrating how, "in conjunction with the prominent gutturals and dominant occlusive consonants, [the] vowels create a mood that is aggressive, volatile, explosive, quite apart from attributions of meaning to individual words and lines" (*Modernism and Negritude*, pp. 236–37). His thorough reading of this poem, which we both agree is seminal to Césaire's corpus, offers much that illuminates and completes the one here. However satisfying Arnold's analysis may be on a formalistic level, it does not account for why the text proceeds in the form of the movements he describes. Here the concept of the subject dilates the humanistic possibility in a way that Arnold's more traditional, thematic "hero" cannot. Similarly, Arnold's brilliant reading of the verse "j'omphale," in light of the Hercules-Omphale myth, elucidates the heroic resonances in an earlier version of "Corps perdu," without being able to confront the textual functioning in the definitive text of the poem.

The anaphoric assertiveness of "moi qui" that punctuates the first seven lines of the poem like a tom-tom seems to place the subject in a position of security from the beginning. There is a beastlike, bellowing, braggadocio quality to the self's identification with the earth, its islands, its rivers ("Zambèze"), its monsoons. This "moi" is qualified by all parts of speech: substantively, adjectivally, verbally, adverbally. Such qualification heightens the all-encompassing, omnipotent affect/effect. But what is the function of the disjunctive pronoun, since at this point the poet switches selves in mid-text so to speak, the "moi" ceding its place to the "je"? What changes with the introduction of the true grammatical subject pronoun? A clue lies with the language that the "je" employs when it first intervenes. Its expression of fatigue and its desire for retraction stand in direct opposition to the language of the "moi." The "moi" seems to have overextended itself to the point of becoming an alienating fiction, which provokes a regressive reaction in the text reminiscent of the last three strophes of Rimbaud's "Le Bateau ivre." But in "Corps perdu," this moment is metamorphosed into a new beginning for the poem and the subject.

The subject modulates from the overexposed, narcissistic status of being topographically and meteorologically identified with the earth to the more private wish for self-nullification inside the womblike oneness of the earth's open "v's":

Je voudrais être de plus en plus humble et plus bas
toujours plus grave sans vertige ni vestige
jusqu'à me perdre tomber
dans la vivante semoule d'une terre bien ouverte.

The desire for loss of self is accompanied here by a wish for amnesia as well, a wish to leave no "vestige," either corporeal or textual. The attitude of the subject to its past as text and as history is important to this study. Paradoxically, the impulse toward dissolution and forgetting is initially the sine qua non that allows the self to explore poetically the various possibilities of its constitution. Throughout Césaire's poetry, we can read the dynamic of the subject in terms of the dialectics of projection, rejection, and introjection. The subject uses the text as that Lacanian mirror that simultaneously promises and denounces the image of completeness to the self. The very title of the poem speaks to this dichotomy.

Let us return to the now amorphous subject of the text. Protected by its privileged, "inside" position, we see that it is free to effect those substitutions based on desire. The signal for desire here is the use of the conditional tense:

Dehors une belle brume au lieu d'atmosphère serait point sale
chaque goutte d'eau y faisant un soleil

This magic new world is characterized by an erasing of all difference, a fusion
of opposites where, perhaps, even one's blackness might go unnoticed. Compare this with Rimbaud's poem "L'Éternité":

Elle est retrouvée.
Quoi?—L'Éternité.
C'est la mer allée
Avec le soleil.[5]

Césaire elaborates on Rimbaud by furthering the association into "soleil"
= "nom" = "le même pour toutes choses" = "RENCONTRE BIEN TOTALE"
and thereby deconstructs the classical interpretation of the poetic process as
one that renames the universe as part of the creative act. This deconstruction
is not a given factor for Césaire, but, rather, something with which his poetry
is constantly struggling. It is the interface between his modernity and his African heritage. For there is the temptation of the demiurge, the magician, the
voodoo shaman to acquire and exert power in terms of renaming. This temptation is the major subject of the "Nommo" chapter in Jahn's book, *Muntu*. He
uses Césaire's poetry as an illustration of the Bantu belief in the force of the
poetic word:

> All magic is word magic, incantation and exorcism, blessing and curse.
> Through Nommo, the word, man establishes his mastery over things. . . . Nam-
> ing . . . produces what it names. . . . Every word has consequences. Therefore
> the word binds the muntu. And the muntu is responsible for his word.
> The force, responsibility, and commitment of the word, and the aware-
> ness that the word alone alters the world; these are characteristics of African
> culture. . . .
> According to African philosophy man has, by the force of his word, domin-
> ion over "things"; he can change them, make them work for him, and command
> them. But to command things with words is to practise "magic." And to practise
> word magic is to write poetry. (pp. 132–35)

But at this moment in "Corps perdu" we are dealing with a different kind of
magical wish, one that seeks not the power to individuate and individualize
through renaming but more a correspondence between all names and all
things. Césaire envisions it as a "RENCONTRE BIEN TOTALE." Capitalizing this

5. Rimbaud, "L'Éternité," "Fêtes de la patience," p. 160.

wish is a form of straining to unite signifier and signified, to abolish difference, and to establish plenitude through proclamation, through the language
of desire.

This approach is closer to the surrealistic credo as put forth by André
Breton in the *Second Manifeste du Surréalisme* of 1930, a credo which Césaire himself quotes in "Poésie et connaissance":

> Tout porte à croire qu'il existe un certain point de l'esprit d'où la vie et la mort,
> le réel et l'imaginaire, le passé et le futur, le communicable et l'incommuni-
> cable, le haut et le bas cessent d'être perçus contradictoirement. Or, c'est en
> vain qu'on chercherait à l'activité surréaliste un autre mobile que l'espoir de
> détermination de ce point.[6]

If we look at the imagery in the poem following "RENCONTRE BIEN TO-
TALE"—the passive submission of the self to sensuality, the wish-fulfillment
conditional tense, the scrambling of epistemological categories in favor of the
primacy of the imaginative faculty—all these point to the surrealist inspiration and praxis:

> si bien que l'on ne saurait plus qui passe
> ou d'une étoile ou d'un espoir
> ou d'un pétale de l'arbre flamboyant
> ou d'une retraite sous-marine
> courue par les flambeaux des méduses-aurélies
> Alors la vie j'imagine me baignerait tout entier
> mieux je la sentirais qui me palpe ou me mord
> couché je verrais venir à moi les odeurs enfin libres
> comme des mains secourables
> qui se feraient passage en moi
> pour y balancer de longs cheveux
> plus longs que ce passé que je ne peux atteindre.

This is another kind of "corps perdu." Yet a counterforce is at work simultaneously; it surfaces in the last line of the quotation above. It represents another
instance in the quest for the self, one that does not succeed in eluding consciousness through synesthetic dissolution but that is troubled by an inability
to define the past. The fatigued subject near the beginning of the text would
like, simply, to be "sans vestige," to be blessed with what Nietzsche calls the
"impossible" for modern man, that is, the ability to forget.[7] Thus the confession by the surrealist self that is haunted by "ce passé que je ne peux at-

6. Breton, *Manifestes du surréalisme*, pp. 76–77.
7. Friedrich Nietzsche, *The Use and Abuse of History*, pp. 5–6.

teindre." The difficulty lies in the fact that the subject can neither forget nor remember. This undeniable presence/absence of the past in the present will burst forth in the text with the full, violent force of an obsession, like the return of the repressed. Here the intrusion of the past, both unremembered and unforgettable, serves as a pivotal deconstruction of the poem's surrealist moment.

The subject, which just a few lines earlier was content for the time span of desire to bathe passively and luxuriously, assuming the sexualized, horizontal position of "couché," allowing himself to be palpated or bitten, playing object to "life's" subject, penetrated by perfumes, hastily rises to consciousness. It gathers up assurance by conjuring with the powerful imperative voice and the possessive adjective and pulls up out of its dream state to a vertical position, addressing "les choses" as if concretizing might serve as a corrective to the amorphous, floating world of desire. The depth of "la retraite sous-marine" with its womblike resonances gives way to a figure of water as surface and wave. It grows in force as it comes crashing in to shore, searching to drop anchor.

"Racines" is a privileged image throughout Césaire's poetry, as are the trees they hold fast, since they provide the satisfaction of belonging to a place, counteracting the painful truth of *déracinement*. Here, the combined image "racines ancreuses" erases the logical boundaries between sea and earth, thus conveying even more powerfully the search of this "corps perdu" for a place "où se prendre."

> Choses je sonde je sonde
> moi le porte-faix je suis porte racines
> et je pèse et je force et j'arcane
> j'omphale.

This seems to be a cry of assertion, victory, aggression, and despair all at once. As Césaire himself once said of Rimbaud: "Paroles mémorables, de détresse et de victoire." [8] The need to find a place for the self among things, to penetrate, to take root, to plunge into the very navel of inner being and outer universe all converge in the intensity of these verses. The surrealistic ideal of the undifferentiated "RENCONTRE BIEN TOTALE" quickly dissolves into inadequacy. It is a textual moment where the subject is fighting against arbitrariness. This desire for assertion may be contrasted to the passive, neutral function of being the transmitter of meaning for the other. In the subtle modification of meaning between "porte-faix" and "porte racines" lies a linguistic

8. "Poésie et connaissance," p. 115.

possibility for freedom. The self attempts to redefine its being and its liberty by effecting a conversion from the syntagmatic to the paradigmatic axis. As "moi le porte-faix" the subject is suppressed, oppressed. But by transforming "moi" into "je suis," and by subverting the verb "porter" so that it carries the desired object and not the other's burden, the subject acquires verbal force, verticality, and potential for action.

We can expand on this notion of the polysemic weight of the verb "porter" by comparing its use in another text from *Cadastre:*

> Maître des trois chemins, tu as en face de toi un homme qui a beaucoup porté.
> Depuis Elam. Depuis Akkad. Depuis Sumer.
> J'ai porté le corps du commandant. J'ai porté le chemin de fer du commandant.
>   J'ai porté la locomotive du commandant, le coton du commandant. J'ai
>   porté sur ma tête laineuse qui se passe si bien de coussinet Dieu, la machine,
>   la route—le Dieu du commandant.
> Maître des trois chemins j'ai porté sous le soleil, j'ai porté dans le brouillard,
>   j'ai porté sur les tessons de braise des fourmis manians. J'ai porté le
>   parasol, j'ai porté l'explosif j'ai porté le carcan.[9]

Here the referent is the slave past, with Césaire as slave, recounting the uses and abuses to which he has been subjected as carrier, underlined by the final, ironic touch where the verb "porter" as transport shifts to denote wearing, thereby clinching the slave's imprisonment.

In "Corps perdu" the subject is struggling to appropriate both meaning and being from the verbal noun, "porte racines," before it is mysteriously "ramené." The urgency of the self's sounding, emphasized by the repetition and the hastened rhythm of "et je pèse et je force et j'arcane / j'omphale" reveals a subject desperate to get it all down, to drop anchor. All these urges unite in the wonderful neologism "j'omphale." The subject is abbreviated through loss of its vowel, thereby merging into the verb as one word. The subject/verb stands rooted to the middle of the page like an umbilicus, surrounded by space on either side, curiously tight and vulnerable at the same time, pressing for finality as its phonemes resonate closely with "je triomphe." The umbilical cord is, after all, the first root and also the first experience of severance, *déracinement,* castration.

The poem might have ended here, but that would have represented an isolating, personal solution. It gives way to the more painful compulsion on the part of the subject to identify with something bigger than itself, to relate to some whole. Some pain must be reaccounted for as the umbilicus is unveiled

---

9. "Depuis Akkad depuis Elam depuis Sumer," *Cadastre,* p. 37.

as wound with the rhetorical question "ah qui vers les harpons me ramène."
The harpoon, the "porte racines," becomes the harpooned. The wild beast of
the beginning of the poem, "moi qui poitrine ouverte," is revealed to be a
human prey, as in so many of Césaire's other texts.

What prompts this dramatic reversal? The subject veers from the victory of
"j'omphale" to an excruciating question to a confession of weakness in just
three lines. This is comparable, dynamically, to the *Cahier,* with its constant
turbulent turnings on itself. In terms of the dramatization of the subject, it is
close to Baudelaire's self-image in the poem "L'Héautontimorouménos":

> Je suis la plaie et le couteau!
> Je suis le soufflet et la joue!
> Je suis les membres et la roue,
> Et la victime et le bourreau![10]

However, the difference between the two poets resides in the attitude of the
self in language. For Baudelaire remains within the controlled parameters of
ironic self-distance. Césaire, on the other hand, is forced beyond the stance of
self-irony by a more violent identification: the image of the self as "nègre"
which he must inevitably confront. We must ask then if the confession "je suis
très faible" is a judgment of what came before in the text, of the effort at a
certain kind of self-definition? Or is it rather that the poetic virtuosity of
"j'omphale" is the very condition that gives the poet the possibility to continue, to face the weakness? A certain amount of ego strength is necessary
before he can willingly resubject himself to the harpoons and relinquish the
textual victory of "j'omphale."

The throbbing, penetrating "je" of a few lines earlier reverts to the more
passive role of message bearer for the other. But here we are speaking of the
other of the self. "L'inconscient est le discours de l'Autre," says Lacan.[11] Repeating messages that require deciphering, "choses très anciennes," the subject whistles vaguely familiar but still incoherent words. Is this a need to allow
past history, be it biological, psychological or sociological, to be articulated
through the subject? The "je" hisses back through the primitive, unconscious
archetypes of phallic serpents and uterine "choses caverneuses," touching
the regressed, fragmented discourse of primary process thought: "Je or vent
paix-là." It arrives, finally, at a kind of nonimage of itself where an amorphous, bestial quality is our only indication of facial trait:

10. Baudelaire, *Les Fleurs du mal,* p. 85.
11. See, for example, Lacan, "Subversion du sujet et dialectique du désir," *Ecrits,*
p. 814.

et contre mon museau instable et frais
pose contre ma face érodée
ta froide face de rire défait.

We have reached degree zero in the text—a moment where the subject is recomposing, starting from yet another "corps perdu," admitting to its vulnerability and lack of definition. As contrasted to the beginning of the poem, the subject is now working toward a new constitution, from the inside out.

This is a quiet moment, one of intimacy, almost of peace. We must explore this in conjunction with the interruption of the "tu" into the text at this point. Whom is the subject addressing? Who is the alter ego, recognized as alter, but invited to become same? Is it woman, or some warped narcissus reflection, or a shadow that has been haunting the text since its inception? This is the first instance of the actual splitting of the self into "I" and "you." The recognition of the division is the condition of the desire for unification and identification between the two parts of the self. The text articulates this recognition by use of the surprising syntax of the imperative "pose" which is flanked on either side by the symmetrical repetition "contre mon museau" and "contre ma face" and the symmetrical but opposite "ma face," "ta face." These echo the first line of the poem entitled "Mot": "Parmi moi / de moi-même à moi-même" (*Cadastre*).[12]

For my purposes here, "contre" is richly ambiguous, since it denotes both next to and against, thereby containing within itself the very tension between separation and identification. The use of "face" instead of *visage* serves to amplify this dialectic, since it carries the associations "faire face" and "face à face." The quiet resolve of the command, the hushed "rire défait," the closeness of the faces almost merging is, textually, the calm before the storm. The primitive self has gathered its forces tightly enough to face the ugly truth of its mirror image. The beast groans in painful recognition:

Le vent hélas je l'entendrai encore
nègre nègre nègre depuis le fond
du ciel immémorial

The beast proves to be a metaphor for alienation, ugliness, marginality, but also potential brute force. Coming to terms with the beast in himself means confronting negritude for Césaire. The truth at the far end of suffering in all his poetry is the image of the "nègre." Unleashing the unconscious through poetry leads back to the slave and, it is hoped, to his *déchainement*. This is the past the subject was striving to attain earlier in the text yet staving off at

12. See discussion of this poem below.

the same time. It explodes with all the force of a revelation. Without assuming this image of the "nègre," the poetic self is not whole, the text is blocked. Its painful recognition, however, provides liberation. The poem itself, then, is the locus of this drama, the subject's reenactment, through poetry, of enslavement and freedom. In this way, the historical is assimilated to the personal, and the personal opens out onto something larger, more meaningful, than itself.

The poet is responsible for bringing the subject back toward the harpoons. The depth of the wound to self-esteem must be sounded with new poetic instruments if it is to be both defined and healed in the same text. Certain poems do not find a way out of this personal hell, but "Corps perdu" is successful. The brutal repetition of the word "nègre," and its situation between the definite future of "je l'entendrai" and the vertiginous space/time past of "depuis le fond du ciel immémorial," attest to the all-pervasive nature of negritude once it is recognized. The challenge for the subject now is to transgress and transcend this self-image.

We have seen in Benveniste that the self is constituted poetically through a positing of the other, the "tu" from which it can then be differentiated. At this point in the poem, however, it is the indirect allusion to the enemy, l'autre, in terms of "ce fou hurlement de chiens et de chevaux" (notice how bestiality is thrown back onto the other), as well as the inclusion of the "tu" in a solidarity of suffering, "notre poursuite toujours marronne," that affords the subject its true voice.

To the wind that howls "nègre" the subject will speak with a volcanic eruption in language that echoes the first line of the poem, "moi qui Krakatoa." In contrast to the end of the text, the anaphoric "moi qui" of the opening lines now appear as fictional, external instances of the self. Here the true grammatical subject "je" functions in an effort to fuse self, word, and action from within, competing, like Demosthenes, against the wind:

mais à mon tour dans l'air
je me lèverai un cri et si violent
que tout entier j'éclabousserai le ciel
et par mes branches déchiquetées
et par le jet insolent de mon fût blessé et solennel

    je commanderai aux îles d'exister

It is difficult for the reader to remain insensitive to these lines. Their power derives in part from the satisfying solution they offer to certain problems posed in and by the text. The self-reflective structure of "je me lèverai un cri" is significant because it articulates a self-contained coming of age in language—"un cri." The "cri," one of painful triumph, is the one Césaire shouts for all his people who are "à côté de leur vrai cri" (*Cahier*). The "cri" then explodes like a volcano, bursting forth from the closed circuit of "je-me," opening out onto the vast sky. This sky, earlier the unremitting reminder to the subject of the bitter "vertige" of "le mot nègre," is now transformed into a screen on which the self ejaculates its new victorious message.

The volcanic and onanistic metaphors are intertwined with the theme of poetic discourse throughout Césaire's poetry. The cluster represents what Charles Mauron calls "métaphores obsédantes."[13] Yet here the victorious "cri" has its source in "mes branches déchiquetées" and "mon fût blessé." While the "racines" earlier in the poem prepare and prefigure the image of self as tree, the castrating adjectives are surprising. Can we read the urgent quest for roots in the middle of the poem as an effort to defend against this castration? When in the text did it become inevitable? And how does this "corps perdu" become *sujet retrouvé?* The possibility for this transformation occurs at the moment when the self is impaled on the harpoon of its coming to consciousness as "nègre." By introjecting this phallic aggression, by assuming this negative image of self to the point of identifying with the castrated image of the "nègre," the poetic subject can be free to turn this image around, to reinvest it with a positive value, to reaffirm itself. As Césaire says in "Barbare," "et nos faces belles comme le vrai pouvoir opératoire / de la négation."[14]

Julia Kristeva, in "Poésie et négativité," points out that it is the privilege of poetic discourse to be able to affirm, negate, and negate this negation within a single articulation. This is a useful idea to bear in mind as we read the final lines of "Corps perdu." The last words, "je commanderai aux îles d'exister," draw their authority for creation and their urgency for presence from the truth of castration.

A kind of magical, mythical substitution is at work here whereby it would be possible, in some projected future, to account for and date the origin of the existence of "les îles" at the very moment of "Corps perdu." The myth could read something like this: "Once upon a time there was a poet who was willing to sacrifice himself for his black people, and the scattered limbs of his broken body became our islands."

The subject, having poetically rediscovered the parts of its castrated self, can then choose to rescatter them metaphorically in the matter of "les îles." The words of the last line stand alone, thrown down onto the page like islands

13. Mauron, *Des Métaphores obsédantes au mythe personnel.*
14. Césaire, "Barbare," *Cadastre,* p. 56.

strewn across the sea. The use of the future tense leaves the text humming with potential yet frail at the same time. We can juxtapose this to the image in the *Cahier,* "ce qui est à moi aussi, l'archipel arqué comme le désir inquiet de se nier" (p. 65). Of course, this erasing is always a possibility. But the subject has offered itself as collateral in this poem. Such phoenix-like sacrificial substitution is worthy of Christian iconography. For this brief textual moment the poetic voice acquires the power of a god with dominion over earth and word. The poem closes on an opening, with a true grammatical subject sublimating its fragmentation, changing its world through poetry.

In the poem "Mot," the text focuses on the very stuff of poetry, the word.[15] The self-referential quality of the title has significance for the subject as well, since the word under consideration here is specified as "le mot nègre." For Césaire as poet, the relationship of the subject to negritude passes necessarily through language. It is in the text that this relationship is constituted, and in the text lies the possibility for its transformation. If we agree that the derogatory connotations that adhere ordinarily to the word "nègre" are those imposed by the structure of the hierarchical relationship that obtains between the white man and the black man in the colonial situation, then a commitment to negritude must somehow articulate a way of changing that relationship. In the poem entitled "Mot" the subject plays the role of an exemplary model for that change by risking its self for the cause in question, by allowing the word to take its place. The "moi" of the text is quite literally supplanted by the "mot," the latter becoming the real grammatical subject of the poem in the last and longest strophe. The subject willingly subordinates itself to the signifier, espouses poetry for better or for worse, rather than attempting to establish a self outside of it. The textual motivation for this acceptance is located within the subject itself. As we shall see, the subject finds itself as lost, clinging to something that no longer permits it to get its bearings.

But the rhetoric of the subject's subordination to the word is problematic, articulating a desire for both death and meaning, a death by meaning, and a meaning by death.

How can we trace the relationship of the subject to the "mot nègre"? A clue lies in the metonymical equivalence between "Mot" as the first title in the reedited collection of "Corps perdu" and the placement of the "moi" at the beginning of the poem "Mot." A text that calls itself "word" and immediately engenders a divided subject suggests the phonemic wordplay that we are about to propose and that will facilitate our reading of the poem.

As noted, "mot" comes to be substituted for "moi" as the subject of the

15. Césaire, "Mot," *Cadastre,* pp. 71–72. See Appendix.

poem. This change is brought about textually by the transformation of the "i" in "moi" into the "t" in "mot." The "i" (no bilingual pun intended here) is a graphic figure for the divided subject, the "corps perdu," the severed self, that, when subordinated to the "t" of the "mot," is reunited with itself. The "t" connects the stem to the dot of the "i," intersects them, thereby binding them together. Lest this observation seem somewhat arbitrary, let us invoke semantic support in the text for the same idea. The subject that conjures up the "mot" in the principal clause of the first stanza is indeed inviting the word to mediate between it and itself, as if to put an alienated subject and its self in touch with each other:

Parmi moi
de moi-même
à moi-même

.   .   .   .
vibre mot

The word is called upon to fill in the gap, the lack (the "i" is also a castration figure).

Further evidence that it is a life-and-death issue between the "moi" and the "mot" is manifested in the rhetorical connection between the subject's last "death wish" in the second strophe and the birth of "le mot nègre" in its first apparition in strophe three:

et que me clouent toutes les flèches
et leur curare le plus amer
au beau poteau-mitan des très fraîches étoiles

.   .   .   .
le mot nègre
sorti tout armé du hurlement
d'une fleur vénéneuse

The blackish poison of the curare plant relates it semantically to "fleur vénéneuse" that produced "le mot nègre." Since it is armed, it can be endowed with "toutes les flèches" and no letter resembles an arrow more than the letter "t." In other words, the "t" nails the "i" and the "mot" pins the "moi" to the "beau poteau-mitan des très fraîches étoiles." If we try to imagine a person bound to a mast, it would have a configuration similar to this.

But is this really a death wish on the part of the subject? Keeping in mind that "flèches" rhymes with "fraîches," one must return to the beginning of the poem to question the status of the subject. The first verses of the text describe the parameters of the subject, elaborating a divided internal space. Then the text proceeds to displace that idiosyncratic subject outside of any usual spatial deployment, "hors toute constellation." Last, the subject is imagined as clinging to something undefined, indeterminate, disembodied both verbally and corporeally, already in the process of dying:

en mes mains serré seulement
le rare hoquet d'un ultime spasme délirant

In short the subject contains an almost-nothing. Confused as it is between being an inside and an outside, perhaps it is the very notion of subject that is dying. Or, in the context of "le mot nègre" that punctuates the latter third of this poem, perhaps it is an intertextual reference to the *Cahier*, "je dis hurrah! la vieille négritude progressivement se cadavérise" (p. 143). What is evident at least is that the subject is at a critical, pivotal point, susceptible to metamorphosis. It passes from container, from the defining force of something no longer valid, through the intermediary of the incantation "vibre mot" to the desire to be contained by the word, within the word.

The first line of the second stanza, "j'aurai chance hors du labyrinthe," is indented, thus related graphically to the initial line of the poem, "parmi moi." The "labyrinthe" from which the subject seeks escape is the one traced by itself in the text, one of the mirror images in which it is somehow lost, "parmi moi / de moi-même / à moi-même." What it calls for then is a new way of relating to itself, of defining itself. Linguistically, the subject can seize itself as object. This requires passing through a signifier, a self-imposed constraint, perhaps a self-imposed alienation, but one that offers a way out of the duality of the Imaginary.

plus long plus large vibre
en ondes de plus en plus serrées
en lasso où me prendre
en corde où me pendre
et que me clouent toutes les flèches
et leur curare le plus amer
au beau poteau-mitan des très fraîches étoiles

The economy of such an enterprise demands an apparent self-sacrifice in exchange for participation in a limitless identification. Yet the risk of the endeavor signals a kind of death for the subject, without the guarantee of rebirth, strangulation without expression. The potential compensation for the risk, however, is that the productive wagon of the subject, to misquote Emerson, can be hitched to a new star. The desire is not to die, then, but to be regenerated, reproduced as a new value. The subject sees containment as an apprenticeship for the infinite. The word is invoked to harness the subject's unknown powers, to utilize them even at the cost of the subject's life, "c'est à force de périr." By accepting the need to devalorize the concept of the self, the subject liberates the transformative force of the word and grants the signifier its primacy.

The surprise and suspense of the text is that in the third stanza, the grammatical subject "je" (or "moi") seems indeed to have perished. "Le mot nègre" is substituted as subject and becomes a model for the process of production, since it engenders its own "free associations." The subject's relinquishing of those dying yet inhibiting values, and of its exigency in its relationship to the category of the self in the first stanza, are the conditions of the possibility of the takeover of the signifying chain. "Le mot nègre" takes on a life of its own as it becomes subject and no longer object of the subject's command. In its latter form the identity of its signified was repressed. Only half of the phrase functioned on the conscious level for the self. It is the subject's persistent address to poetic discourse, to rhythm and repetition, to self-less-ness and word-hood that releases "l'essence même de l'ombre," the unconscious "nègre" of the "mot," the alienation in the Symbolic. The effect of the appearance of the full phrase "le mot nègre" is shocking, violent, revelatory. It is as if the subject itself were unconscious of what sound the vibrating word would produce and yet compelled, at the same time, to invoke it. The word echoes in the text with a force all its own, capable of infinite repetition and unusual association.

This bringing of the word "nigger" into the light of day of new constellations is analogous to the subject's exposure on the mast of fresh stars in the second stanza. And as the subject hoped to be redeemed by this martyrdom, so "le mot nègre" is redeemed from its usual connotations. Stripped of its clichés, it reveals new possibilities.

The images that emanate from "le mot nègre" are disparate, their forms dissimilar, the attitudes that they convey juxtaposed. This shock is meant to jolt the reader, the other, perhaps the enemy, into the kind of vigilant stance vis-à-vis his usual acceptance of the connotations behind the word, and it testifies to the kind of textual production at which Benjamin believed all progressive art should be aimed. In discussing Brecht's epic theater in the essay on "The Author as Producer," Benjamin differs between reproducing a situation and discovering it (pp. 220–38). The object here for Césaire is to deconstruct the habitual denigrating ideology that subtends the word "nigger" by making words themselves into a "claquement de balles."

In its repetitions the text emphasizes the "word" as much as "nigger." Because the two are always articulated in conjunction with each other, "nigger" is at one and the same time defused and reinforced. The metaphors that develop out of the repetitions expose the whole gamut of networks whose contradictions are the very source of poetic recuperation. They reveal suffering, narcissism, aggression, disgust, pain, oppression, and, most important of all, the liberating function of metaphoricity itself:

le mot nègre
sorti tout armé du hurlement
d'une fleur vénéneuse
le mot nègre
tout pouacre de parasites
le mot nègre
tout plein de brigands qui rôdent
des mères qui crient
d'enfants qui pleurent
le mot nègre
un grésillement de chairs qui brûlent
âcre et de corne
le mot nègre
comme le soleil qui saigne de la griffe
sur le trottoir des nuages
le mot nègre
comme le dernier rire vêlé de l'innocence
entre les crocs du tigre
et comme le mot soleil est un claquement de balles
et comme le mot nuit un taffetas qu'on déchire
le mot nègre
    dru savez-vous
du tonnerre d'un été
     que s'arrogent
       des libertés incrédules

Does a significant, diacritical difference intervene at some point in the repetition here? Can we trace a progression in the catalogue? The first three sets of images that follow "le mot nègre" are modified by the encompassing "tout," which serves as an expansive device, pushing on the limits of the word. In the first images, a whole history seems to be condemned. Fragments of that history which acted upon the word to produce its Athena-like birth, "sorti tout armé du hurlement d'une fleur vénéneuse," are reenacted in the images that follow, evoking *déracinement* and the painful aspects of the black slave's life. But they are still only fragments. These initial de-repressions of

"le mot nègre" unleash violent images which do not cohere into a single signified that can then be interpreted and forgotten. Is this fragmentation threatening or liberating? Or rather, is the menace transformed into the source of
liberation the way, psychically, repetition can uncover the repressed, bring it
to consciousness, and thereby eliminate its threat? What one can say at least is
that repetition brings metaphor to identify itself consciously as such, and this
self-consciousness has a dialectical and liberating function. We said that the
subject in the beginning of the poem gave itself over to the "free associations"
of "le mot nègre." One could say that it was subjected to the word and to
whatever it might reveal in the way of pain, suffering, horror. But a change
occurs in the text with the intervention of the signal for comparison and substitution, the "comme."

    What is significant about this is that it permits "le mot nègre" to jump into
the liberating realm of the surreal. Until this point, "le mot nègre" has been
associated with memories of alienation, humiliation, and victimization. Now
the associations take on a dangerous, menacing tone, transforming pain into a
device of poetic aggression. The threatening tone that the two surrealist metaphors share seems to stem from the possibility of positing the "comme" as if,
in acknowledging resemblance, "le mot nègre" had already begun asking for
some kind of reparation. The intuitive gesture on the part of the subject in the
beginning of the poem, which consisted of exhorting the word to vibrate
against itself no matter what the outcome for the subject, bears fruition. If the
word "nigger" can evoke so many different emotions, memories, images, can
it not then command the very possibility of substitutability? Is this not the
bridge that leads to poetic freedom, at least? Perhaps that very word that is a
shorthand for pain can be used to inflict it? This would represent a satisfying
thematic symmetry in the poem. The subject that internalized its victimization by the arrows of the word "nègre" in the "death wish" imagery of the
second stanza discovers a liberating justification when the same word exhibits
outwardly aggressive tendencies. By having merged with the "mot," the
"moi" can participate metaphorically in this externalized hostility.

    The transformation that the signifier "comme" itself undergoes at the end
of the poem supports such a reading. Initially indicative of the self-conscious
intervention of metaphor, it serves now as a way of introducing and embracing
a whole new analogous structure that permits "le mot nègre" to function as a
word among words, special, different, but equal:

    et comme le mot soleil est un claquement de balles
    et comme le mot nuit un taffetas qu'on déchire
    le mot nègre
        dru savez-vous

du tonnerre d'un été
    que s'arrogent
        des libertés incrédules

What are the consequences of the poem's reinvestment of "le mot nègre"? It has made the word itself a source of poetry, in the same way that sun and night are. Its contiguous positioning next to these two grants it a new participatory status among the most basic of structuring elements: day and night, light and dark, white and black. Moreover, the menacing possibility attributed to "soleil" and "nuit," the shocking sounds and the tearing, are assimilated into the force of "dru . . . du tonnerre d'un été." Most important of all, however, is the way in which the word "nigger" reconstitutes the other and a plural subject at the end of the poem. The power that the "mot" of the poem projects is appropriated triumphantly by the plural subject, itself surprised at the metamorphosis into freedom that the poem engendered by redeeming "le mot nègre." In fact, the subject is so transformed that we barely recognize it as such. It is only the anthropomorphic adjective "incrédules" that leads us to a reading of "libertés" as a figure for subjects.

The other, reader, friend, enemy, is postulated simultaneously in the menacing address "savez-vous," whose form is partly affirmative, partly interrogative, and whose seme articulates the gravity of this new-found freedom: it is a knowledge with which one must contend. This address to the other, the capacity to address the other with "le mot nègre" in its potent form, compels a recognition of the new relationship to the word. The reversal is the source of the "libertés incrédules." The subject takes the liberty from the other, as it were, by reappropriating the word "nigger" which is so often thrown at it. It does this for everybody, as the plural indicates. Does the "incrédule" suggest a doubt on the part of the subject concerning the nature of authority and freedom that the text has just granted it? Or because the poem might well have been the locus of the subject's dispersion, disappearance, is the attitude of incredulity more like that of the prisoner sentenced to death who finds in the sentence itself the possible commutation to freedom? If the latter seems more likely to us, it is because it is inscribed within the more general notion of poetic constraint as constitutive of freedom for the subject. In a poem such as this, where a liberation is effected for the subject, it is because the text engenders it. Such freedom does not exist prior to the text. It is the chance the subject took in the beginning of the poem by textualizing itself, by submitting to "le mot," to the Symbolic. The subject then reemerges transformed, freed from the word, and not vice versa. But the liberating effect of this transformation is dialectical, since the word, in all its new poetic possibilities, can then be recuperated by the subject and utilized as a positive defining tool in its struggle for identification. The very metaphoricity by which the subject is designated at the end of the poem, "des libertés incrédules," and its plural form, as well as the pride connoted by the verbal attitude of "s'arroger," attest to the successful binding of the subject with the ideals of negritude: poetic reinvention utilized to reveal black solidarity and identity.

This leads us to an investigation of the problems posed textually when negritude is transformed from an end term to a figural revolving door. The subject can turn inward on itself or outward toward that enlarged version of negritude that is *engagement*.

5. The Subject and *Engagement*

> Bref, si j'avais à définir l'attitude du poète de la négritude,
> la poésie de la négritude, je ne me laisserais pas désorien-
> ter par ses cris, ses revendications, ses malédictions. Ses
> cris, ses revendications, je ne les définirais que comme
> une postulation, irritée sans doute, une postulation impa-
> tiente, mais en tout cas, une postulation de la fraternité.
>
> Aimé Césaire,
> "Discours sur l'art africain"

THIS "postulation de la fraternité" is at the heart of those texts that attempt to define the dimensions of the relationship between the poet and his readers, particularly, his "people." But the poet and the reader are not constants that can be counted upon to be identical with themselves, to function in a consistent manner in relation to each other. The scene of each text is different, the drama of the subject in the process of effecting an identity is played differently in each poem. It is important to investigate these distinctions, to question each text on its own terms instead of accepting a monolithic definition of *engagement*. Who is the speaking subject? Is he poet, hero, comrade, martyr, slave, pedagogue, bard, rebel, lover, madman, desperado? Is his self-definition at odds with what the text articulates about him? What are the results of such a conflict for the subject's status? And who is the public to whom the subject attempts to address himself? Are they allies, comrades, "nègres," slaves, wretches, countrymen, lovers, cowards, enemies, whites, Europeans? Is there, perhaps, no public at all? Is the public dead, or deaf, or indifferent? Does the subject encounter solitude instead of fraternity in a so-called engaged text? Is the textual intention didactic or ironic? Is the statement one of unity or solitude?

The two poems that will be discussed at length in this chapter articulate some of the postures of the subject/public relationship, and the textual complexities reveal the difficulties the subject encounters in attempting to transcend itself, despite an authentic "postulation de la fraternité."

The title of the poem "Hors des jours étrangers" defines a spatial/temporal tension that is itself a revelatory locution.[1] The utilization of a preposi-

---

1. Césaire, "Hors des jours étrangers," *Ferrements*, pp. 81–82. See Appendix. See

tion of place as applied to the temporal "jours étrangers" is indicative of the kind of breaking out of habitual linguistic categories that is operative in the Césairian text concerned with liberation. A new space must be created, "hors," which will constitute a freeing from the alienating "jours étrangers." The very title, then, is a call to disalienation. Can the text propose a "how"? Many fundamental questions cluster around the inside/outside polarity representative here of the black conflict, not the least of which is the poet's self-imposed relationship to the people for whom he speaks. The text means to point to a way out of yet another "ferrement," yet its complexities are such that it cannot help but be the "ferrement" as well as the condition of liberation from it. Time, translated by the verb tenses, is of the essence within the compact spatial frame of the poem. The present tense is alienated time, "les jours étrangers," to which the poem opposes a mythical past time, on the one hand, and a desired, hoped-for future time, on the other.

The word "étrangers" of the title is immediately contrasted with the first line of the text, "mon peuple." This contrast defines the opposition between strange/intimate or other/self. Yet self must be examined scrupulously. It is not the subject of which we have been speaking in the usual sense. The text does not articulate "je"; rather, it is a collective self with which the speaking subject seeks to identify. The use of the possessive adjective "mon" is a statement of solidarity, belonging, intimacy, comradeship. However, this opening line is disposed on the page like a salutation addressed by a speaker to his public. A certain distance is fixed, spatially, between the poet and his people. Is it necessary for him to step outside, "hors" as it were, in order to be the teacher, the prophet, the poet? Does this act consequently isolate the subject from exactly that collectivity with which it yearns to identify? In other words, is the non-articulated "je" at a remove, alienated, as it were, from the alienation of the "tu" that is the ostensible subject of this text? For neither does the poem articulate a "nous." It is desired, implied in "mon peuple," but it disintegrates with the question "quand . . . germeras-tu . . . ?" We observe this here because it seems that the binary opposition self/other is cómplicated by a more ambiguous triangulation that breaks down into I/you/they, where the poet's identity fluctuates vertiginously and where, ironically, he is haunted by the possibility of exclusion in all directions.

What mitigates this threat of isolation is the tone of the text, which is pained, implicated, lucid, supportive, imploring. By asking "when," the future is assumed. The posed question is coextensive with the articulation of possibility. Desire is described. What the interlocutor wants for his people is well defined, yet reading it as a question serves to shift responsibility for ac-

---

also Aliko Songolo, "*Cadastre* et *Ferrements* de Césaire: Une nouvelle poétique pour une nouvelle politique," p. 154, for a less dialectical reading of this poem.

tion onto the people themselves. Rather than imposing a future, which would only be repeating "des jours étrangers," the text asks for it. The phrasing of the question is not without significance. The first question reiterates the self/other opposition, although for the moment the self to be defined is that of the "tu": "quand / hors des jours étrangers / germeras-tu une tête bien tienne sur tes épaules renouées." The hammerlike repetition of the "t" sounds gives the shifter a stability, establishing the validity of the existence of the "tu" and of all that might belong to it. The humorous, homey plant metaphor reinforces this impression of existence because of its form, that of an active, transitive verb, and because of the positive connotations which Césaire gives to all that is growing and rooted throughout his poetry. Not only is the self-hood of the "tu" valorized, its capacity to be, recognized, but its capacity to have, also, is emphasized in the possibility of its reclaiming a bodily wholeness for itself, head and shoulders, as it were, through the possessive adjectives "tienne" and "tes." In a text grappling with the problems of alienation on both an individual and a collective level, this esthetic perception of wholeness is an important step on the road to self-hood. We see this in our discussion of the poem "Corps perdu" and in Lacan's reflections on the "corps morcelé" in his essay "Le stade du miroir." [2]

We must not ignore the slavery referent here, either, since the slave's body, as well as his labor, was alienated from him. But more important, head is the figure for the locus of thought. On an ideological level, then, the question translates into "my people, when will you be able to think for yourselves?" It points to the recurrent opposition between white values and black values, which is one of the constants of the colonial conflict. The entire colonial superstructure is aimed at brainwashing and assimilation. And since this is all attempted through propaganda, that is, message and language, liberation must be effected through discourse: "et ta parole." The suspension of these three signifiers at the end of the strophe forces the text to a momentary halt. We must read both backward and forward. Is "parole" another object of "quand . . . germeras-tu"? Or the subject, with an elliptical verb, of "le congé dépêché"? Either way, it becomes, momentarily, the instrument of disalienation, for imagining it and articulating it permit the assumption of the signified, that is, the sarcastic image of the reversal of the existing order:

et ta parole
le congé dépêché aux traîtres
aux maîtres

If the poet, however gently and indirectly, denounced his people in the previous strophe through the question about change and growth, he now names

2. Lacan, "Le stade du miroir," *Ecrits I,* pp. 93–95.

the enemy with vehemence, rhyming "traîtres" and "maîtres," identifying the criminal and the oppressor as one. Yet the text does not dwell on their description. They are quickly "dépêchés," so that the poem can move on to the promised land and to a further exploration of the relationship between poet and people.

In a verbal formulation that attempts to change reality before the reader's very eyes, the text states the objectives of the desired reversal:

> le pain restitué la terre lavée
> la terre donnée

The purity and transparency of these goals, the basic earthy quality of these images, and the simplicity with which they are articulated are a seduction, a kind of fortification and nourishment for what follows in the text. For without this positive hope held out as if within reach, re-presented as if present, the "tu" could not withstand being subjected to the humiliating definitions that follow without the poet becoming identified with the aggressor. The text is predicated on the assumption that proffering an image of possible completeness and self-sufficiency to "mon peuple" is what permits its further progress into the reality of alienation. Even as it denounces, it uses the interrogative form and the future tense as a possible escape exit from its own horrible vision:

> quand
> quand donc cesseras-tu d'être le jouet sombre
> au carnaval des autres
> ou dans les champs d'autrui
> l'épouvantail désuet

"Jouet" and "épouvantail" are both reductive, subhuman, reified images. The adjectives "sombre," with its racial overtones, and "désuet," with its implication of inadequacy and anachronism, add insult to injury. The humiliation and mockery achieve a subtly grotesque level which attests to the power of the introjected racist image on the part of the black that is part of the colonial dialectic. For it is Césaire who is describing his people here, and not the enemy.

"Carnaval" and "champs" cover the two poles of leisure/work, both of which are alienated from the people. They have nothing, they are only what they are for the others. The structure of the question posed by this strophe can be read, "When will you cease to *be* that which others *have?*" Liberation, then, must involve a de-reification, a reappropriation of self from the other. But the first condition of such an act is confrontation with the power of the other. The battle for self-hood (the people's) cannot be waged in the linguistic vacuum of "tu," "tienne," and "tes" but must define itself against the enemy, "l'autre." Perhaps this necessity accounts for why the "other," present only through implication until now, here appears twice in the same stanza, as "autres" and "autrui."

The question "when," emphasized by repetition and reinforced by the impatient locution "donc," functions structurally as a device that attempts to coerce the people into a dialogue and, therefore, into existence. The active participation that the question is meant to elicit from the answer is short lived, however. For, not surprisingly, the answer is an alienated one, "demain." If this response were accepted, the text would be blocked. "Demain" is not a promise but a rhetorical mystification, related, intratextually, to the alienated "jours étrangers" and not to the visionary future tense. But the poet does not allow the otherness of the people's response to arrest the signifying chain. The answer is incorporated into the next question, restored as a signifier. Instead of standing as a finalized signified, "demain" slips back to the other side of the bar, thereby engendering a new stanza. It is preceded by the poet's challenge, "à quand," which puts it into question, and followed by his protective cushioning, "mon peuple," which has a paternal quality. A small, textual battle has just been won over the word "demain." As the sole intrusion into the text of the voice of the people, "demain" is pivotal. Initially, it stands alone, as the voice of the other, alienated, the "jouet" or the "épouvantail." But the temporary victory of the poem resides in the way in which "demain" is recuperated. It is flanked verbally on either side by Césaire's two faithful poetic instruments, interrogation and reaffirmation of solidarity.

It is in the light of these remarks that we read the two lines that follow:

la déroute mercenaire
finie la fête

The combination of battle and economic vocabulary of "déroute mercenaire" is ambiguous but not incongruous, given the dialectical tensions within the text. Is the "déroute mercenaire" a positive or negative value? We can read it as the further alienated fate that awaits the people if they accept "demain" at the face value accorded it by the forces of capitalist power, that is, the infinite delay of gratification in exchange for exploitation. So can the text instruct the people from the new vantage point with "demain" as floating signifier?

On the other hand, we can read "déroute mercenaire" as the desired reversal to be accomplished by the people, for which the poet waits impatiently. For the text can also be read as "à quand . . . la déroute mercenaire." "Demain" would then become the moment of revolt against the existing order. According to this reading, the next line in the text, "finie la fête," would then echo the "carnaval des autres" in the sense of "the party is over." However, "finie" could also modify "la déroute mercenaire," giving us an elliptical ablative absolute construction that would read "une fois la déroute mercenaire finie / il y aura la fête." Or is "finie la fête" a declaration of a sheer act of will on the part of the poet, a result of his growing frustration and impatience with those he is trying to change? If so, it might account for the change in tack that the text takes at this point. It seems that these ambiguities in meaning as well as in temporal sequences and relationships can be traced to the seminal importance of "demain," which is still being weighed in the balance.

The poem itself does not seem able to resolve this ambivalence through the question and answer method, for after this strophe, after the "déroute," the problematic is rerouted through two other poetic devices characteristic of the Césairian text. These two new modes of articulation are used in alternation, as if they were meant to dialogue with each other. We must question the relationship of this purely structural dialogue to the one that the text attempted to articulate between poet and people. Does it deconstruct it? The people are still called upon repeatedly but in a different way. The poet relates to them in a different way. Is this a retreat? Is the text striving to differ from itself so as to break out of the earlier stalemate, one more "ferrement" broken? The poem posits an alternative here as nature and the cosmos intervene: "mais la rougeur de l'est au coeur de balisier." It is nature that is evoked as a source of hope and strength when the dialectics of oppression are blocked.

This solution is inherited from the Rimbaldian text. Following closely on verses obsessed with temporality and the reinvention of time, this line is strangely atemporal. It stands without a verb, suspended on the page, hovering with potential yet out of time. Dawn, heart, red, and flower are condensed within this image, where the native "balisier" flower is perceived as a source of hope, the dawning of a time not yet unfolded. In the name of this timeless future, the past is now called up:

peuple de mauvais sommeil rompu
peuple d'abîmes remontés
peuple de cauchemars domptés
peuple nocturne amant de fureurs du tonnerre
demain plus haut plus doux plus large

The poet has changed his position in relation to the people. This is manifested textually by the elimination of the direct address to "mon peuple" with its indicting interrogation. In its place, we have what constitutes a kind of mythical epic catalogue. The poet calls upon the collective past of the people, reciting, like an African *chantre,* their common history and heritage. This is not a glorious, glorified recitation but rather a list of feats constituted by the surpassing of defeats. In this sense, it is a gloss on the poem's difficulties. The references to the suffering endured and overcome are abstract, but they encompass physical, moral, psychological, and emotional functions. Alienation is revelatory of the human. As each offense is listed, it is neutralized poetically by the past participle of the verb that follows. In each case, the semantic value of the verbal adjective is its power to negate what it modifies, and its temporal value is its power to relegate to the past: "mauvais sommeil rompu," "abîmes remontés," "cauchemars domptés." This incantation is meant to function as a recalling of victorious struggles. It is not a nostalgic regression into a past fiction but a call to arms. The poetic strategy of this device is more complex than a first reading would indicate. On one level, this reminder of strength gives the text its impetus to constitute the people in their own terms and not in alienated terms. But it is through this catalogue that the poet is reinstated indirectly as being the necessary authority for the people's discourse. They are named in the intimacy of night, desire, and primitive cosmic forces, but such naming is dependent upon him and therefore points to the problematic relationship that obtains between poet and people. Would true liberation obliterate the text entirely?

In the next line, "peuple nocturne amant des fureurs du tonnerre," nocturnal stands as a value in contradistinction to "jours étrangers" as a possible time/place that is the people's own, an identity that they can valorize positively, having wrested it from the immobilizing black/white polarity and reinvested it with new meaning. One thinks again of Sartre's analysis of the cultural ramifications of the ways in which black and white are valued within the colonial context.

This reversal of the hierarchy is the condition for a further probing into negritude, characterized in these lines as a being at one with the powerful, primitive forces of night and nature. In *Les Damnés de la terre,* Frantz Fanon insists that decolonization must be a tabula rasa phenomenon (p. 5). In Césaire's text, it often translates into an unleashing of the forces of nature, simultaneously destructive and regenerative, as in Rimbaud's prose poem "Après le déluge." By placing the "people" in contact with its "nocturnal" self (which is achieved, textually, by the contiguity of the two words in the line), by going beyond their alienated present condition as described earlier in the poem to the deeper, constant present of the real self, Césaire attempts to arrive at the untapped resource of identity that allows the text to make the transition to the "devenir" of a different "demain." The text prepares for this by its forceful rhythm and the intensity of the incantatory repetition of "peuple." The key notion of "demain" in the poem is here the end term of a temporal progression that has traced the people's triumphs in the past, their coming to terms with self-hood in the present, and the desire for a newly invested tomorrow which will be a future disalienated. In conjunction with what we have said above, "demain" is now qualified as if it stood, itself, "*hors* des jours étrangers." "Plus haut" and "plus large" are spatial characteristics with a symbolic and moral value connoting freedom, breathing space. They are not descriptions ordinarily applied to time. "Plus doux" stands in opposition to "fureurs du tonnerre," as the real goal that is beyond violence. "Demain" must be reinvented in order to be disalienated. Reversal of the habitual time/space categories is one way of reappropriating the signifier.

This upheaval is carried over into the last two lines of the text:

> et la houle torrentielle des terres
> à la charrue salubre de l'orage

The storm images were released by the thunder of a few lines before, and the deliberate misapplication of "houle," a sea word, to "terres" reinforces the whole ambition of this text which aims at liberation through reversing the existing alienated order. It certainly serves to make the poetic word, at least, "plus haut" and "plus large." Like the line "mais la rougeur de l'est au coeur de balisier," these two lines are atemporal, without verb. Furthermore, the conjunction "et" which initiates them is a structural callback to the "mais" of that line. All three lines share a common nature thematic, although the last two are far more violent. They seem to be of a piece, to call to each other across the stanza of the "peuple." At the same time, they frame this stanza with their potential eternal present which is waiting to become, to be conjugated into the future. The protective, hopeful potential of dawn, the challenging potential of the storm, can be related structurally to the framing of "demain" by "à quand . . . mon peuple." Does this mean that the text pivots around a lack, remains incomplete, waiting for the people to supply a verb, that is, action, to the poet's vision? To extend a textual metaphor, he has done the groundwork for them, cleared the land. By resorting to the imagery of cosmic phenomena, he has supplied answers to his own metaphysical questions, but what price has been paid in the process? The reader ("le peuple"?) is left to evaluate the significance of the natural forces imagery. It is gratifying imagery in terms of the semantic integrity of the text. The "houle torrentielle des terres / à la charrue salubre de l'orage" represents one alternative response to the question concerned with growing ("quand . . . germeras-tu une tête bien tienne"), with purifying the earth ("la terre lavée / la terre donnée"), with reappropriating the fields of labor ("quand . . . cesseras-tu d'être . . .

dans les champs d'autrui / l'épouvantail désuet"). Yet having to resort to these figures is tantamount to a by-passing of the relationship between the poet and the people within a text where such a relationship seemed indubitably inscribed. This Prospero's position is an isolated one compared to the poet's initial stance which was meant to enlist his people in a dialogue. The text seems to point to a lapsus. The poet as individual voice has somehow failed to merge with a social universal as desired. Instead, he substitutes a cosmic universal.

If we read back in the poem, we see a subtle shift in the distance between poet and people when he chooses to become their *chantre*. They cease to be "mon peuple" and become, instead, fictionalized, endowed with other attributes. Ironically, this functions as a distancing factor. The poet sacrifices a certain selfish intimacy to a greater, more outward-turned cause for his people, only to find himself condemned to a certain solitude. This result is comparable to certain moments of the *Cahier* and even more apparent in the character of the rebel in Césaire's tragic play, *Et les chiens se taisaient*.

"L'orage," as pathetic fallacy, is both tears and rage. Can we read the poet's call to nature in its excessively violent form at the end of the poem as a kind of compensation for failure to engage his people as comrades in battle? It would not be a vindictive response, which is uncharacteristic of the dynamic between poet and people, but rather a frustrated response meant to keep failure at bay. For, as we have noted, the poem ends with a picture of sweeping cosmic reversal which is curiously suspended between its initial conjunction and its lack of verb.

This inconclusive conclusion cannot mask the fact that the text is articulated in such a way that it deconstructs its own thematic, that what began as a striving toward a relationship, a "postulation de la fraternité," ends in a subsuming of that relationship to the greater, external forces of nature. Such a transformation puts into question the nature and the possibility of the poet/ people relationship. Yet this poem is the very opposite of a blocked or solipsistic text. It triumphs because it finds a way to continue beyond the disillusionment of an unfulfilled relationship. It can speak to and for the people despite their reluctance. And although it must reach beyond their limits, it knows no limits of its own. The status of the text as arm is ambiguous, but the depth of the poet's commitment is not.

In contrast, let us turn to a text where the subject is so alienated that it is not even in touch with its desire to be "la bouche de ceux qui n'ont point de bouche," a text of strangulation, inhibition, confusion, and despair, where the subject is locked within its "ferrement."

The poem "Grand sang sans merci" is characterized by the depersonalized, impersonal "pays," as opposed to the "peuple" of "Hors des jours étrangers."[3] And yet, even a first reading of the text immediately reveals the idio-syncratic mapping of this "pays," which is highly subjective. No subject is actually posited here, but the poem painfully addresses itself to the reason why. The "pays" is the corollary of the subject frustrated in its efforts to ar-ticulate and realize its desire to be. We are looking at what Césaire calls in "Séisme" an "intime patrie," as evidenced by the anthropomorphic quality of the descriptions of the "pays."[4] The reader is thrown into an atmosphere of psychological and moral stagnation and suffocation through imagery that powerfully fuses internal and external landscapes. Implicit in this fusion, however, is the text's statement of a con-fusion as to where the boundaries of self and other lie. If the "pays" is a metaphorical mirror image of the self, what is it saying of the original it reflects when it speaks of laceration, frag-mentation, frustration, and, especially, silence? The text speaks of silence that is inability to speak, silence that is an injunction against speaking, silence that is forgetting, silence that is frustration, silence that is nescience. But it also speaks of silence that is compulsion to speak as the least guarantee of existence, like those Beckett characters who proclaim, "I cannot go on; I'll go on." And therefore it says that speaking silence is at once the most alienating and the most humanizing of acts.

What can this text, which is perhaps the most desperate and pessimistic in all of Césaire's oeuvre, tell us about our problematic? Can there be a subject of a statement in which the subject does not know it is speaking, does not pro-nounce "I"? And what sort of relationship obtains, if any, between this indi-vidual subject and others in the next to the last line of the poem where self and selves fuse in a daring identification and a last effort at designation and inser-tion of someone(s) who could be identified as "articulators"? The subject per-ceives itself as cruelly compelled drive, which the title, "Grand sang sans merci," indicates, and as stifled word. Present though absent, it hovers around the edge of the text, haunting each infinitive verb that does not manage to insert itself into history through the choice of a conjugation. This impotence, this alienation from both a subjective and a historical time, this inability to choose, or even to know what to choose, and the merciless self-conscious exi-gency to state this, these all are the subject of the *enoncé*, if not of the *énon-ciation*. The energy of the text is both its "grand sang," "the blood of the poet," the "cavale rouge," and the fact that it is "sans merci," that it is a com-pulsion, a scrutinizing, a silence-saying.[5]

3. Césaire, "Grand sang sans merci," *Ferrements,* pp. 23–24. See Appendix.
4. Césaire, "Séisme," *Ferrements,* p. 10.
5. Cf. "mais il y a ce mal," *Ferrements,* p. 26: "de ce sang du mien tu diras / que toujours au seuil il buta de son galop amer."

The status of the "pays" in this poem is problematic and therefore illuminating in a certain way. Without being human, it is dehumanized. It
stands as a figure for both the individual, the poet, and for the collective oppressed. The question to be asked here is whether the spatializing concept of
the "pays," despite the despair that it paints, might permit a more effective
poetic mediation between subject and people than the direct address of "Hors
des jours étrangers"? Or, on the contrary, is the expansion that the concept of
"pays" facilitates thwarted textually, thereby throwing the subject back onto
its nonself, with nothing left to do but accuse? Only the text can answer these
questions.

The poem has three stanzas: the first is a description of the "pays," the
second the litany of defeat, and the third an interrogation. In this brief structural sketch we can already call attention to the fact that "defeat" is placed in
such a way so as not to have the last word in the poem. It is important to
realize this in order to be able to read beyond the obvious despair of the text,
to the possible reasons for it which the poem is attempting to articulate.

The first strophe of the text alternates between descriptions of resigned,
generalized hopelessness and those, more directed, of identifiable anger
against the offense of existing conditions. This oscillation cannot but be indicative of the struggle of two instances of the subject, however grammatically absent it may be. In the same way, a text that goes on to constitute
itself in defiance of the injunction of its opening line, "du fond d'un pays de
silence," is also thematizing on poetry. Although not initially apparent, perhaps, the text is dealing with the possibility to be, in language, for both the
subject and the poem.

What, then, characterizes this "pays"? On the one hand, concrete images
of death and destruction: "d'os calcinés," "de sarments brûlés," "d'orages";
on the other hand, abstract images of moral and psychological anguish: "de
cris retenus," "de désirs irrités," "de naufrage," "de soif," "sourd," combined with images of the futility or impossibility of any gesture that would
release who or what from the block. The self-enclosed form of this first part
of the poem gives it a textual look of what we call "islandness." It also likens
the "pays" to the poem, which is self-imposed constraint. The "pays" and the
text are therefore apt images for each other.

The tensions and confusions between internal and external reveal a concern with the nature of limitation, closure, even imprisonment, which is completely consistent, despite its paradoxical quality, with a subject that is simultaneously inhibited and amorphous.

Moreover, there is an ever increasing tension between active and passive
that reveals the intensity of the relationships between subject and other, subject and text. If the subject is grammatically absent from the poem yet pas-

sively identified with the "pays," the active forces of oppression are equally absent. Some hostile force is responsible for calcifying the bones, burning the vines, stifling the screams, erasing the traces on the sand, blocking the exits, imprisoning the steed. But the question is whether this aggressive force is external or internal, in terms of the subject and the text. It is more than a metaphorical castration fantasy, for the text has produced and induced its own crisis *qua* text. It has reached a point of no return. Everything has been burned, cut, uprooted, drowned, gagged, blocked, silenced. The silence of the sand, punctuated by parentheses to dramatize its inarticulability, its impossible yet insistent insertion into the poem, stands as a metatext of absence, in search of the human writing trace and of animal prints. The sand is the page. But the "cavale rouge" is also a figure for the subject, and the text it attempts to write does not constitute it. Rather, it leaves uncertain traces of frenetic trapped energy, at the mercy of currents that threaten to annihilate them.

In this stanza of the poem, the impersonal grammatical subject in the form of the reflexive inserts itself once, hesitatingly, only to denounce its own project contemptuously:

> où s'agripper est vain à un profil absurde de mât totem et
> de tambours

We insist on these lines because of their structure. The infinitive offers the possibility of a gesture that is rendered immediately invalid by the judgment of the absent self. The image reaching out (or back, in time) echos the other figures in this first part of the poem which speaks of "une inquiétude de branches / de naufrage." But the intense urgency connoted by the verb "s'agripper," coupled with the devalorization of the act as "vain," leads to a violent indictment of past symbols or solutions: "un profil absurde de mât totem et / de tambours." So there is no going back, no escape here through nostalgia or extratextual identification, no roots that hold fast. And there is no exit, either, only the powerful image of a savage force trying desperately to break out of its boundaries:

> d'un pays de cavale rouge qui galope le long désespéré
> des lés de la mer et du lasso des courants les plus perfides

"Perfides," like "vain" and "absurde," is the value judgment of the absent subject's superego. Between the frustrated drives that characterize the first part of the poem, and the harsh criticism of any gestures that might transform existing conditions, the subject is completely inhibited and repressed. It has no place where it can set itself up.

The litany that follows and makes up the second stanza of the poem provides a response to this deadlock. The confrontation of defeat comes from "du fond d'un pays," but here it is the desert that is imagined, in all its vastness, as opposed to the insular quality of the "pays." Like the "pays," the defeat/desert is an externalization, a spatialization, at once alienating and liberating for the subject. But a different drummer is at work here. The funereal rhythm and phonetic repetition of this strophe signal a death that makes the images of the first strophe seem almost lyrical in comparison. Does defeat comment on, describe the first stanza, or, rather, is it the admission of defeat that engenders the stanza? Certainly its disposition in the middle of the poem, its capitalization, and its repetition ensure its central position, so that we are forced to come to terms with it as the subject is trying to. What, then, is this "Défaite"? It is not an event. It is, etymologically, an un-doing. In its place at the center of the text, it can un-do what preceded it and thereby initiate the questions that constitute the third stanza of the poem. This shift is effected through the image of the "désert grand" in contradistinction to the "pays" and, also, through the evocation of a natural force not yet called upon in the poem: the wind. The wind, devastating to be sure, worse than the worst, "plus sévère que le Kamsin d'Egypte / siffle le vent d'Asshume," can be read nonetheless as a possible force of recuperation. It provides a momentary exile from the constraints of the "pays." The exotic, oriental names of the winds open up a space, even if it is a destructive one. The intense heat of "le vent d'Asshume" may have created the landscape of the first part of the poem, but it can also destroy it. Such destruction "creates" a tabula rasa in the poem. It is no longer possible to continue in the same way. The poem will not proceed from the more internalized landscapes of self-doubt. In the face of Defeat, the inevitable question must be posed: What can be done? It is Rimbaud's question, too, "Comment âgir, ô coeur volé?"[6] It is not only a question of what to do. Inextricably entwined with it are the questions, for the subject, of how to be, what to speak, and for whom. "Défaite" is the undoing of all the certitude that the subject longs for in support of its gestures, be they poetic, personal, or political.

The posing of the questions that constitute the third stanza of the poem articulates a problem, not a solution, namely, the difficulty of making any clear-cut, differential choice. Can a subject hope for a meaningful, univocal, positive self-consciousness as long as it is condemned to be both oppressor and oppressed? The possibility to be, in no uncertain terms, would require a dialectical synthesis that is perhaps beyond the scope of the problem posed in this particular poem. Unconstituted then, the only modes of expression open

6. "Le coeur volé," *Œuvres*, p. 100.

to the subject are those that speak of its doubt: the form is interrogative, the mood passive, the subject elided, the verbs infinitive, the complements of the object indeterminate: "de quelle taiseuse douleur choisir d'être le tambour et de qui chevauché." The economy of these verses is extraordinary, for in them is resumed the whole project of both subject and poem. In the structure of the question lies also the possibility of its deconstruction. The infinitive of "choisir," and "choisir d'être," preceded by the question "de quelle," gives the illusion of the freedom of a choice that is then negated as the choice is shown to be textual obligation, and obligation to language, further complicated by the oxymoronic quality of being the "tambour . . . d'une taiseuse douleur."

The word "tambour" appears for the second time here in the poem but in such a different context that it merits our attention. Its first insertion in the text, as noted, comes under the aegis of vanity and absurdity:

où s'agripper est vain à un profil absurde de mât totem et
de tambours

What is different about "tambour" in the question "de quelle taiseuse douleur choisir d'être le tambour" is that a transformation is taking place, an internalization. When the old myths, the old gods, the old values, even the old rhythms, no longer correspond to internal reality or suffice to represent it, then a substitution must occur whereby the subject and its discourse, here the poem, become both internal and external reality. The possibility of a referential escape has been suppressed, thereby focusing the poem much more intensely on the problematic of the absent subject. This is not a lesson imposed upon the text from the outset but, rather, the very process, the very confrontation of the text itself. The question asked is really the fundamental one of the ambiguous status of the subject in the poem. Here again we invoke Rimbaud, and his definition of the alienation of the subject:

C'est faux de dire: Je pense. On devrait dire:
On me pense. . . . Je est une autre. Tant pis
pour le bois qui se trouve violon . . .[7]

In other terms, this is Lacan's subjection of the subject to the signifier.[8] If we compare the two instruments that Rimbaud and Césaire "choose" as figures for the poetic self, we see to what extent the unconscious overdetermination that structures discourse corroborates their statements. For Rimbaud's text

7. "La lettre du 13 mai 1877," p. 344.
8. See, for example, Lacan, "Subversion du sujet et dialectique du désir."

speaks of the violin and Césaire's of the "tambour." This self-same "tambour," which proved insufficient earlier in the poem as cultural object, is nonetheless the signifier through which the subject's message, albeit opaque, perverse, and painful, cannot help but be articulated. It is a locus, a rhythm, yet not sufficient to constitute a consciousness, despite the illusion implied by "choisir." Even the title of the poem, "Grand sang sans merci," in speaking the biological drive rather than the poetic, echos this relentless quality over which the subject has no control.

What the self and the text share is that they are both, coextensively, "tambour" and "taiseuse douleur." What is this question if not a comment on the first part of the text, incorporating into the third stanza of the poem what was a self-contained externalization? The question is formulated in such a way that active and passive, internal and external, subject and object seem to merge, or, in Breton's terms, "cessent d'être perçus contradictoirement." [9] The subject is subsumed by the text, and only the text can say it. The whole first stanza of the poem, rhythmed as it is by the anaphoric "du fond d'un pays," is itself the "tambour" of "une taiseuse douleur," that of the "pays." For Césaire takes this "pays" very much to heart, as can already be seen in the *Cahier*. No matter what reading we give to this image, it is a constant throughout the oeuvre, and most often functions as a device that permits an extension of the inner landscape from which the poems can then close in, in ever narrowing circles, to a more concise confrontation with the self. Perhaps the "Défaite" for the subject here is the inability to bridge the gap between self and "pays," to be constituted by or represented in the "pays," even for the short space of the poem, in a way which would be disalienating. The "Défaite," as undoing, is what reduces the possibility of an active, willful gesture into a passive, doubtful one. Thus, the "cavale rouge qui galope le long désespéré / des lés de la mer et du lasso des courants les plus perfides," not having found an outlet for its force, is trapped and transformed into "de qui chevauché." The wild, unbridled steed of freedom is enslaved into the domesticated, dominated instrument of the other's will:

> de quel talon vainqueur
> vers les bayous étranges
> gémir se tordre

However, the "talon vainqueur" that extends the image of "chevauché" is not necessarily an external, referential other. As self-imposed suffering (another "ferrement"), it nonetheless has the liberating function of forcing the

9. Breton, "Second manifeste du surréalisme," in *Manifestes du surréalisme*, p. 77.

"cri," which in turn becomes the condition for a possible articulation of the self. The scream, as so often in Césaire, has both an aggressive and an immediately reconstructive value. Moreover, it is a collective subject that is posited. Its assertion in the next to the last line of the poem, combined with the unusual use of the past narrative tense, the image of the barrier limit being broken down, and the repetition of the signifier "nuit" used differently each time, all combine to form a signifying system that defies a unified, unambiguous reading of the last part of "Grand sang sans merci." Our purpose here is to expose these antagonistic forces of signification to see what they tell us about the struggle of the subject.

The entire meaning of the text in time is put into question by the past definite of "installa" which implies a pretextual history. This implication invites some kind of casual reading that might account for the self-recriminating tone of the last stanza of the poem. Yet it would constitute a mystification to look for an error outside of the text. Let us look closely at the last strophe:

de quelle taiseuse douleur choisir d'être le tambour
    et de qui chevauché
    de quel talon vainqueur
    vers les bayous étranges
gémir se tordre
crier jusqu'à une nuit hagarde à faire tomber
la vigilance armée
qu'installa en pleine nuit de nous-mêmes
l'impureté insidieuse du vent

There is not a progressive worsening of conditions here, only a shift in emphasis from description to interrogation. Yet a coherent relationship obtains between the two. The otherness of the self is now imaged in terms of battle, in terms of a relationship of domination but an intratextual and intrapsychic one. We cannot point easily to a concrete, obvious reference to the objective colonial power struggle as the source that arms this battle. The poem itself is the product of the struggle for freedom. The syntactical ambiguities of the last stanza reveal great incertitude, but they also provide the possibility and even the necessity of rereading. The dispossession or the resubjection of the subject to the other is not only the effect of defeat. Being victimized by the force of the "talon vainqueur" generates a suffering that in turn liberates the scream and its destructive force. We can even read "gémir se tordre / crier" as complements of the infinitive "choisir" and its questions, so that the self is seen as a will-to-suffer but lacking the assurance that such suffering will break through the stalemated oppositions that the poem sets up.

If we read in reverse from the end of the poem, the "vent" of the last line wafts back over the text to the second part, echoing "le Kamsin d'Egypte" and "le vent d'Asshume." Its message of defeat is characterized as "impureté insidieuse." It is responsible for the construction of "la vigilance armée," a defense against deepest despair, "en pleine nuit de nous-mêmes." A highly condensed drama is being enacted at the end of the poem. Only here is the plural, collective subject articulated at all, although not as a grammatical subject. Still, the text implies that the concept of "nous-mêmes" was once operative and that the particular textual tragedy is also a universal one. The barrier of "la vigilance armée" is in some sense the last vestige of a communal accord. It is a defensive barrier. The question that must be asked of the text is why this stance is stated in such confusion. For it can be valorized either positively or negatively. The primary process gestures and articulations of "gémir se tordre / crier" that threaten to break down the defenses of "la vigilance armée" can be read, we have seen, as a positive unleashing of internal, unconscious forces that would serve as a possible corrective against the erroneous, poisonous, internalized acceptance of defeat. Like the "courants perfides" of the first part of the poem, the wind is qualified by negative moral qualities. In this way, the desperate response of "ourselves," which was one of armed vigilance, was an incorrect one, because it implies that defeat was triumphant. Is the acceptance of defeat the cause for the difficulty of this text? Does it precede the poem rather than result from it? Is the poem attempting to articulate a subject that might triumph over this preordained defeat?

These questions open the way for other readings of the last stanza. For in laying bare the mechanics of defeat, the poem may be exposing the defense of "armed vigilance" to destruction. As the first and last vestige of "ourselves," this vigilance has a fragility to it, despite its military sound. As a protective response to the winds of defeat, it is perhaps the scene of the last battle for self-hood, a defense that is the only possible offense—"comment âgir, ô coeur volé?" But who or what exactly is the perpetrator of this crime against the collective self? The text does not tell us. It ends with a scathing self-indictment which appears to be misdirected because the self cannot be localized here. Its externalized, aggressive impulses are redirected inward in such a way that they appear as both cause and effect of an ever growing yet undefinable internal trauma. The inability for the subject to know, in a definitive way, even textually, the difference between before and after, is in one sense the real subject of this poem. In a poetic world where these values are susceptible to reversal, where the subject is not necessarily master of its own text but, rather, enslaved by it and subjugated to it, it is not surprising that it does not manage to constitute itself.

The structure of the subject's relationship to its own quest for self-hood in this text is a microcosmic repetition of its alienated relationships in other contexts. Such alienation is articulated in the ambiguous question "de quelle taiseuse douleur choisir d'être le tambour et de qui chevauché." The only way to be is to speak, and vice versa. But these are alienated possibilities. Paradoxically, a required dispossession of the subject is implied in these verses. And even at such a price, there is no guarantee as to in-the-name-of-what the self is being subsumed. Equally paradoxical is the hermetic, collective-self-referential *nostra culpa* that the poem pronounces at the end but that affords no relief because it functions as a "vigilance armée," resisting all those (readers included) who might seek to absolve it. Yet this convoluted confession does identify a community, a collective entity. And it even manages to articulate the logic of its convolution. The "pleine nuit de nous-mêmes" is polyvalent. It appears as lack or vacuum, concavity, supreme permeability, ultimate cowardice that offers no resistance to the invasion of the "impureté insidieuse du vent." This is what we might call its ancient history, the oblique description of an original sin, marked by the definite past. But it is also the converse. The "pleine nuit de nous-mêmes" has become a hard core of blackness, convex, like a huge fist threatening to destroy but cut off from a center on the inside as well as impenetrable from the outside. Like certain characters in Dante's *Inferno,* whose punishment is a formal reflection of their sin, Césaire's "nous-mêmes" are condemned to the Sisyphean effort of trying to defeat their defeat by un-doing it ("dé-faire"): "jusqu'à une nuit hagarde à faire tomber / la vigilance armée." The harsh economy of the text is such that this is the only weapon that might be pitted against the "pleine nuit de nous-mêmes." A vaguely hopeful question is trying to take shape here which would read something like this: "Can we recuperate, through suffering and self-imposed violence, that force which, through our own weakness, we alienated from ourselves by accepting defeat? Can we earn the privilege of being equally responsible for our own disalienation?" But the subject, individual and/or collective, is deprived of the luxury of such an articulation. The questions are fragments, the logic trapped in the vicious circularity of self-doubt, the goals virtually obscured by the pain and despair required to realize them.

The poem is, indeed, a "Grand sang sans merci." The self cannot issue its own exit visa from this "pays" since it has relinquished its authority to the forces of doubt and defeat. Yet by blocking all the exits, it forces an intense confrontation and it articulates a collective implication in the impossibility to be constituted. The speaking subject is on equal terms with the group, no more nor less delineated. It is not set apart from the others by a paternalistic attitude, by affecting a discourse of knowledge, or by any heroic, individual gesture of martyrdom. The subject does not allow itself any privileged stance. Rather, the poem forces it to stand guard at its gates, enacting another "vigilance armée." This excruciatingly honest position has a redemptive feature. The subject, perhaps, is not. But it is also not alone in this Lacanian "manque-à-être." The poem establishes a relationship, however painful, between the self and the selves.

Conclusion

THE UNIQUE difficulties of Césaire's poetry begin to take form as a problematic rather than as a series of discontinuous obstacles to imposing an "interpretation" when we utilize certain conceptual models that allow us to grasp the complex nature of the textual project concerned both with elaborating a discourse of the subject and with exploring ways of mediating between it and a collective form of identity in language. We have seen that what these models share, be they linguistic, sociopolitical, or psychoanalytic, is a common reflection on the relationship between the subject and the other, or the Other. The subject cannot know itself, indeed, cannot articulate itself poetically without simultaneously positing a relationship of otherness. Césaire's poetic texts investigate the various facets of this relationship and experiment with the limitations of its formulation. The relationship can function positively, permitting the subject to identify itself personally, poetically, and communally. Or this relationship can function negatively, revealing the ways in which the subject is alienated, inhibiting it from establishing itself as an integrated unity in language or in history. But these two functions relate dialectically, informing each other and transcending each other, rotating slightly in each poem so as to expose a different dramatis personae.

As has been demonstrated, the subject can be poet, victim, slave, universe, lover, spokesman, nigger, island. The other can be language, oppressor, master, lover, people, poem, country. The thrust that motivates the exposition of these oppositions aims at demystification and rectification. In his *Discours sur le colonialisme,* Césaire says that "la malédiction la plus commune . . . est d'être la dupe . . . d'une hypocrisie collective, habile à mal poser les problèmes pour mieux légitimer les odieuses solutions qu'on leur apporte" (p. 6). These poems, then, seek to restate problems.

Psychoanalytic theory tells us that repetition is an attempt at psychic mastery of trauma. As Césaire moves from the *Cahier* to *Les Armes miraculeuses* and thence to *Cadastre* and *Ferrements,* restating the problems of the alienated subject with an ever sharper discipline, it becomes clear that poetic repetition and difference do indeed serve an integrative function, if only for the time/space of each text. The subject's intense investment in the text, although often articulated in the Imaginary terms of inside and outside, is not only the condition of its constitution. It is the possibility of its liberation. The work of the subject in the text becomes a theme unto itself for both writer and reader.

This acts as a poetic antidote to Fanon's bitter analysis of that liberating aspect of the Hegelian Master/Slave dialectic that is inoperative in the colonial situation because of the Slave's incapacity to free himself in work due to his over-identification with the Master. That from which the subject is by definition excluded by the colonial context is its very subjectivity. Césaire's poetry transforms it into a reading of marginality and a reaffirmation of its esthetic possibilities for the subject. If cultural subversion leads to subjugation, poetic inversion can be utilized as a source of liberation. If colonialism has sought to confine Césaire to his isolated Martinique, he can refine poetic form into the ultimate island—"accommodez vous de moi." If the subject recognizes itself as alienated there, it can define a solidarity in this alienation.

I have stressed throughout that the relationships that Césaire's poems articulate between the subject and its others are dynamic and not static. In the light of the analyses of *engagement* discussed in chapter 1, it should now be evident that the text's commitment to positing shifting relationships is already a form of response to the absolute stagnation and reification imposed by the colonial hierarchy. Poetic discourse offers the subject the option of not conforming to any preconceived model or mode but rather of being formed in it, reborn in it. The underlying risk of language's arbitrariness is, of course, that being can veer to nothingness. But if the process is alienating, it should be emphasized nonetheless that it is process and therefore susceptible to transformation and transcendence. The constraints of form do not offer the subject a guarantee against this arbitrariness, but they do serve a constitutive function when the form is self-imposed. And through the poem the subject articulates the Imaginary that permits it to explore the configurations of identity and difference. The possibility of multiplying oneself, of seeing oneself reflected as one is, would like to be, cannot be, or is afraid to be, which poetic articulation provides for Césaire, is invaluable when measured against a cultural context that imagines the black man as worse than nonexistent.

The problem will always remain of how to make such an experience universally valid and how to utilize it as an instrument of change. But Césaire's text never states anything different. The subject's major discovery in the *Cahier* is that *engagement*, like charity, must begin at home. The text sets as its task a restating of the problem incurred by the politically engaged writing subject; it does not proffer any facile solutions. "Hors des jours étrangers" showed us that a poem that seemed initially to be asking a simple question was of necessity also a reflection on the difficulties of articulating a response.

The vitality of Césaire's poetry springs in part from the subject's determined will not to substitute a new mystification for an old one. This subject, which has nothing, is nobody, tirelessly pursues its investigations of the various aspects of its own dispossession in language. But Césaire utilizes it to liberate affect previously unknown, and its poetic dimension is one of great beauty. The power of the images that are thereby released, and the subject's intense yearning and desire to be identified with a collective unity greater than itself that is thereby revealed, attests to the epistemological function of this activity for the subject: "poésie et connaissance." And, therefore, we might add, liberty.

Our readings show us to what extent the biographical fact of having been born marginal, both in terms of cultural standards lauded by the white man over the black man, and in terms of a peculiar geocentrism insisted upon by the French metropole, contributes to determining those specific imaginary configurations that represent Césaire's "métaphores obsédantes." But Césaire's genius lies to a great degree in the textualization of that marginality by which it is metamorphosed into privilege and, therefore, responsibility. The black subject, condemned by racism to a position of exteriority, finds itself in the unique situation of being able to question and make problematical the very categories of inside and outside, of resemblance and difference. The poetic image, multiply determined as it is, is suited to this task.

Whether Césaire's subject inhabits its text comfortably, or roams its parameters seeking new entrance, or forces its boundaries in an effort to escape, we recognize what Breton characterized as "cette qualité sans cesse majeure du ton" that identifies true poetry.[1] And even when the subject painfully acknowledges its alienation from itself, its capacity to speak only of itself and for itself as alienated, we recognize throughout Césaire's poetic text the subject's profound commitment to change the conditions that inhibit its constitution so that the "horribles travailleurs" to come will find the page and the world less horrible than it did.

1. "Un Grand Poète noir," p. 13.

Appendix

Et moi, et moi,
moi qui chantais le poing dur
Il faut savoir jusqu'où je poussai la lâcheté.
Un soir dans un tramway en face de moi, un nègre.

C'était un nègre grand comme un pongo qui essayait de se faire tout petit sur un banc de tramway. Il essayait d'abandonner sur ce banc crasseux de tramway ses jambes gigantesques et ses mains tremblantes de boxeur affamé. Et tout l'avait laissé, le laissait. Son nez qui semblait une péninsule en dérade et sa négritude même qui se décolorait sous l'action d'une inlassable mégie. Et le mégissier était la Misère. Un gros oreillard subit dont les coups de griffes sur ce visage s'étaient cicatrisés en îlots scabieux. Ou plutôt, c'était un ouvrier infatigable, la Misère, travaillant à quelque cartouche hideux. On voyait très bien comment le pouce industrieux et malveillant avait modelé le front en bosse, percé le nez de deux tunnels parallèles et inquiétants, allongé la démesure de la lippe, et par un chef-d'œuvre caricatural, raboté, poli, verni la plus minuscule mignonne petite oreille de la création.

C'était un nègre dégingandé sans rythme ni mesure.

Un nègre dont les yeux roulaient une lassitude sanguinolente.

Un nègre sans pudeur et ses orteils ricanaient de façon assez puante au fond de la tanière entrebâillée de ses souliers.

La misère, on ne pouvait pas dire, s'était donné un mal fou pour l'achever.

Elle avait creusé l'orbite, l'avait fardée d'un fard de poussière et de chassie mêlées.

Elle avait tendu l'espace vide entre l'accrochement solide des mâchoires et les pommettes d'une vieille joue décatie. Elle avait planté dessus les petits pieux luisants d'une barbe de plusieurs jours. Elle avait affolé le cœur, voûté le dos.

Et l'ensemble faisait parfaitement un nègre hideux, un nègre grognon, un nègre mélancolique, un nègre affalé, ses mains réunies en prière sur un bâton noueux. Un nègre enseveli dans une vieille veste élimée. Un nègre comique et laid et des femmes derrière moi ricanaient en le regardant.

Il était COMIQUE ET LAID,
COMIQUE ET LAID pour sûr.
J'arborai un grand sourire complice . . .
Ma lâcheté retrouvée!

(*Cahier*, pp. 101–5)

115

Le Cristal automatique

allo allo encore une nuit pas la peine de chercher c'est moi l'homme des cavernes il y a les cigales que étourdissent leur vie comme leur mort il y a aussi
l'eau verte des lagunes même noyé je n'aurai jamais cette couleur-là pour penser à toi j'ai déposé tous mes mots au monts-de-piété un fleuve de traîneaux de
baigneuses dans le courant de la journée blonde comme le pain et l'alcool de
tes seins allo allo je voudrais être à l'envers clair de la terre le bout de tes seins
a la couleur et le goût de cette terre-là allo allo encore une nuit il y a la pluie et
ses doigts de fossoyeur il y a la pluie qui met ses pieds dans le plat sur les toits
la pluie a mangé le soleil avec des baguettes de chinois allo allo l'accroissement du cristal c'est toi . . . c'est toi ô absente dans le vent et baigneuse de
lombric quand viendra l'aube c'est toi qui poindras tes yeux de rivière sur
l'émail bougé des îles et dans ma tête c'est toi le maguey éblouissant d'un
ressac d'aigles sous le banian

                                                    (*Les Armes miraculeuses*)

Totem

De loin en proche de proche en loin le sistre des circoncis
et un soleil hors moeurs
buvant dans la gloire de ma poitrine un grand coup de vin
rouge et de mouches
comment d'étage en étage de détresse en héritage le totem
ne bondirait-il pas au sommet des buildings sa tiédeur de
cheminée et de trahison?
comme la distraction salée de ta langue destructrice
comme le vin de ton venin
comme ton rire de dos de marsouin dans l'argent du naufrage
comme la souris verte qui naît de la belle eau captive de
tes paupières
comme la course des gazelles de sel fin de la neige sur la
tête sauvage des femmes et de l'abîme
comme les grandes étamines de tes lèvres dans le filet bleu
du continent
comme l'éclatement de feu de la minute dans la trame serrée
du temps
comme la chevelure de genêt qui s'obstine à pousser dans
l'arrière-saison de tes yeux à marine

chevaux du quadrige piétinez la savane de ma parole vaste
ouverte

du blanc au fauve
il y a les sanglots le silence la mer rouge et la nuit

(*Cadastre*)

Intimité marine

Tu n'es pas un toit. Tu ne supportes pas de couvreurs.
Tu n'es pas une tombe. Tu ignores tout silo dont tu n'éclates le ventre. Tu
n'es pas une paix. Ta meule sans cesse aiguise juste un courroux suprême de
couteaux et de coraux. D'ailleurs en un certain sens tu n'es pas autre que
l'élan sauvage de mon sang qu'il m'est donné de voir et qui vient de très loin
lorsque le rire silencieux du menfenil s'avance en clapotant du fond funèbre
de la gorge de l'horizon.
  Et voilà qu'en cou de cheval en colère je me vois, en grand serpent. Je
m'enroule je me déroule je bondis. Je suis un vrai coursier déplié vers une
éclatante morsure. Je ne tombe pas. Je frappe, je brise, toute porte je brise et
hennissant, absolu, cervelle, justice, enfance je me brise. Climat climats connaissance du cri, ta dispersion au moins s'épanouirait-elle et au-delà de toute
épouvante?
  Cependant telle une chevelure l'âpre vin de fort Kino monte l'escarpement
des falaises très fort jusqu'à la torpeur tordue des coccolobes.

(*Ferrements*)

Corps perdu

  Moi qui Krakatoa
moi qui tout mieux que mousson
moi qui poitrine ouverte
moi qui laïlape
moi qui bêle mieux que cloaque
moi qui hors de gamme
moi qui Zambèze ou frénétique ou rhombe ou
cannibale
je voudrais être de plus en plus humble et plus bas
toujours plus grave sans vertige ni vestige
jusqu'à me perdre tomber

dans la vivante semoule d'une terre bien ouverte.
Dehors une belle brume au lieu d'atmosphère serait
point sale
chaque goutte d'eau y faisant un soleil
dont le nom le même pour toutes choses
serait RENCONTRE BIEN TOTALE
si bien que l'on ne saurait plus qui passe
ou d'une étoile ou d'un espoir
ou d'un pétale de l'arbre flamboyant
ou d'une retraite sous-marine
courue par les flambeaux des méduses-aurélies
Alors la vie j'imagine me baignerait tout entier
mieux je la sentirais qui me palpe ou me mord
couché je verrais venir à moi les odeurs enfin libres
comme des mains secourables
qui se feraient passage en moi
pour y balancer de longs cheveux
plus longs que ce passé que je ne peux atteindre.
Chose écartez-vous faites place entre vous
place à mon repos qui porte en vague
ma terrible crête de racines ancreuses
qui cherchent où se prendre
Choses je sonde je sonde
moi le porte-faix je suis porte racines
et je pèse et je force et j'arcane
        j'omphale
Ah qui vers les harpons me ramène
        je suis très faible
je siffle oui je siffle des choses très anciennes
de serpents de choses caverneuses
Je or vent paix-là
et contre mon museau instable et frais
pose contre ma face érodée
ta froide face de rire défait.
Le vent hélas je l'entendrai encore
nègre nègre nègre depuis le fond
du ciel immémorial
un peu moins fort qu'aujourd'hui
mais trop fort cependant
et ce fou hurlement de chiens et de chevaux
qu'il pousse à notre poursuite toujours marronne

mais à mon tour dans l'air
je me lèverai un cri et si violent
que tout entier j'éclabousserai le ciel
et par mes branches déchiquetées
et par le jet insolent de mon fût blessé et solennel

   je commanderai aux îles d'exister

(Cadastre)

                        Mot

            Parmi moi
de moi-même
à moi-même
hors toute constellation
en mes mains serré seulement
le rare hoquet d'un ultime spasme délirant
vibre mot
            j'aurai chance hors du labyrinthe
plus long plus large vibre
en ondes de plus en plus serrées
en lasso où me prendre
en corde où me pendre
et que me clouent toutes les flèches
et leur curare le plus amer
au beau poteau-mitan des très fraîches étoiles

vibre
vibre essence même de l'ombre
en aile en gosier c'est à force de périr
le mot nègre
sorti tout armé du hurlement
d'une fleur vénéneuse
le mot nègre

tout pouacre de parasites
le mot nègre
tout plein de brigands qui rôdent
des mères qui crient
d'enfants qui pleurent
le mot nègre
un grésillement de chairs qui brûlent

âcre et de corne
le mot nègre
comme le soleil qui saigne de la griffe
sur le trottoir des nuages
le mot nègre
comme le dernier rire vêlé de l'innocence
entre les crocs du tigre
et comme le mot soleil est un claquement de balles
et comme le mot nuit un taffetas qu'on déchire
le mot nègre
        dru savez-vous
du tonnerre d'un été
           que s'arrogent
                des libertés incrédules

                                        (*Cadastre*)

Hors des jours étrangers

mon peuple

quand
hors des jours étrangers
germeras-tu une tête bien tienne sur tes épaules renouées
et ta parole

le congé dépêché aux traîtres
aux maîtres
le pain restitué la terre lavée
la terre donnée

quand
quand donc cesseras-tu d'être le jouet sombre
au carnaval des autres
ou dans les champs d'autrui
l'épouvantail désuet

demain
à quand demain mon peuple

la déroute mercenaire
finie la fête

mais la rougeur de l'est au coeur de balisier

peuple de mauvais sommeil rompu
peuple d'abîmes remontés
peuple de cauchemars domptés
peuple nocturne amant des fureurs du tonnerre
demain plus haut plus doux plus large

et la houle torrentielle des terres
à la charrue salubre de l'orage

(Ferrements)

Grand sang sans merci

du fond d'un pays de silence
d'os calcinés de sarments brûlés d'orages de cris retenus
et gardés au museau
d'un pays de désirs irrités d'une inquiétude de branches
de naufrage à même (le sable très noir ayant été gavé de
silence étrange
à la recherche de pas de pieds nus et d'oiseaux marins)
du fond d'un pays de soif
où s'agripper est vain à un profil absurde de mât totem et
de tambours
d'un pays sourd sauvagement obturé à tous les bouts
d'un pays de cavale rouge qui galope le long désespéré
des lés de la mer et du lasso des courants les plus perfides

Défaite Défaite désert grand
où plus sévère que le Kamsin d'Egypte
siffle le vent d'Asshume

de quelle taiseuse douleur choisir d'être le tambour
                    et de qui chevauché

            de quel talon vainqueur
                vers les bayous étranges
gémir se tordre
crier jusqu'à une nuit hagarde à faire tomber
la vigilance armée
qu'installa en pleine nuit de nous-mêmes
l'impureté insidieuse du vent

(Ferrements)

Bibliography

Works by Aimé Césaire

Books

Cahier d'un retour au pays natal. Translated by Emile Snyder. Bilingual edition. Preface by André Breton. 3d ed. Paris: Présence Africaine, 1971.
Les Armes miraculeuses. 2d ed. Paris: Gallimard/Poésie, 1970.
Soleil cou coupé. Paris: Editions K, 1948.
Corps perdu. Paris: Fragrance, 1949.
Soleil cou coupé and *Corps perdu*. Reedited as *Cadastre*. Paris: Seuil, 1961.
Discours sur le colonialisme. Paris: Présence Africaine, 1955.
Lettre à Maurice Thorez. Paris: Présence Africaine, 1956.
Et les chiens se taisaient. Paris: Présence Africaine, 1956.
Ferrements. Paris: Editions du Seuil, 1960.
Toussaint Louverture. La révolution française et le problème colonial. 2d ed. Preface by Charles-André Julien. Paris: Présence Africaine, 1962.
La Tragédie du Roi Christophe. Paris: Présence Africaine, 1963.
Une Saison au Congo. Paris: Seuil, 1967.
Une Tempête. Paris: Seuil, 1969.
Discourse on Colonialism. Translated by Joan Pinkham. New York and London: Monthly Review Press, 1972.
Cadastre. Translated by Emile Snyder and Sanford Upson. Bilingual edition. Paris: Seuil, 1961; New York: The Third Press, 1973.
Oeuvres complètes. 3 vols. Fort-de-France, Martinique: Désormeaux, 1976.
Moi, laminaire. Paris: Seuil, 1982.
The Collected Poetry. Translated by Clayton Eshleman and Annette Smith. Bilingual edition. Berkeley: University of California Press, 1983.

Articles in *Tropiques*

Césaire, Aimé, and Ménil, René, eds. *Tropiques*. Fort-de-France, 1941–45. Reprint ed. of the complete collection, 2 vols., Paris: Jean-Michel Place, 1978. (All references are to the reprint edition.)
"Présentation." 1 (avril 1941): 5–6.
"Introduction à la poésie nègre américaine." 1 (juillet 1941): 37–42.
"Isidore Ducasse, Comte de Lautréamont." 2 (février 1943): 10–15.
"Maintenir la poésie." 2 (octobre 1943): 7–8.
"Poésie et connaissance." 2 (janvier 1945): 157–70. First reprinted in Lilyan Kesteloot and Barthélemy Kotchy, *Aimé Césaire, l'homme et l'oeuvre*, pp. 112–26. Paris: Présence Africaine, 1973.

124   *Engagement*

Articles in *Présence Africaine*

"Sur la poésie nationale." 4 (octobre–novembre 1955): 39–41.
"Décolonisation pour les Antilles." 7 (avril–mars 1956): 7–12.
"Culture et colonisation." 8–10 (juin–novembre 1956): 190–205.
"L'Homme de culture et ses responsabilités." 24–25 (février–mai 1959): 116–22.
"Hommage à Frantz Fanon." 40 (1ᵉʳ trimestre 1962): 119–22.

Other Articles by Césaire

"Société et littérature dans les Antilles." *Etudes littéraires* 6 (avril 1973): 9–20.
"Discours sur l'art africain." *Etudes littéraires* 6 (avril 1973): 99–109.

Other Works

Almeida, Lilian Pestre de. *O Teatro negro de Aimé Césaire.* Rio de Janeiro: UFF–CEUFF, 1978.
Alquié, Ferdinand. *Philosophie du surréalisme.* Paris: Flammarion, 1955.
Armet, Auguste. "Aimé Césaire, homme politique." *Etudes littéraires* 6 (avril 1973): 81–96.
Arnold, A. James. "*Cahier d'un retour au pays natal:* Reflections on the Translations into English." *Cahiers Césairiens,* no. 3 (printemps 1977): 33–40.
———. *Modernism and Negritude: The Poetry and Poetics of Aimé Césaire.* Cambridge: Harvard University Press, 1981.
Balandier, Georges. "La Littérature noire de langue française." *Présence Africaine,* nos. 8–9 (1950): 393–402.
Baudelaire, Charles. *Les Fleurs du mal.* Edition d'Antoine Adam. Paris: Garnier Frères, 1961.
Benamou, Michel. "Entretien avec Aimé Césaire à Fort-de-France, le 14 février 1973." *Cahiers Césairiens* 1 (printemps 1974): 4–8.
———. "Sémiotique du *Cahier d'un retour au pays natal.*" *Cahiers Césairiens* 2 (automne 1975): 3–8.
Benjamin, Walter. "The Author as Producer." In *Reflections,* translated by Edmund Jephcott, edited and with an introduction by Peter Demetz. New York: Harcourt Brace Jovanovich, 1978.
Benveniste, Emile. *Problèmes de linguistique générale.* Paris: Gallimard, 1966.
Bloom, Harold. *The Anxiety of Influence.* New York: Oxford University Press, 1973.
Breton, André. "Un Grand Poète noir." Preface to *Cahier d'un retour au pays natal* by Aimé Césaire. 3d ed. Paris: Présence Africaine, 1971.
———. *Manifestes du surréalisme.* Paris: Jean-Jacques Pauvert, n.d.; Paris: Gallimard/Idées, 1965.
Cailler, Bernadette. *Proposition poétique: Une lecture de l'œuvre d'Aimé Césaire.* Sherbrooke, Canada: Editions Naaman, 1976.
Case, Frederick Ivor. *Aimé Césaire: Bibliographie.* Toronto: Manna Publishing Company, 1973.

————. "Aimé Césaire et l'Occident chrétien." *L'Esprit Créateur* 10 (Fall 1970): 242–56.

Césaire, Suzanne. "1943: Le surréalisme et nous." *Tropiques* 2 (octobre 1943): 14–18.

Clément, Catherine B. *Le Pouvoir des mots: symbolique et idéologique.* Paris: Mame, 1973.

Condé, Maryse. *Cahier d'un retour au pays natal.* Paris: Hatier, 1978.

de Man, Paul, *Blindness and Insight.* New York: Oxford University Press, 1971.

Depestre, René. *Arc-en-ciel pour l'Occident chrétien.* Paris: Présence Africaine, 1967.

————. *Minerai Noir.* Paris: Présence Africaine, 1956.

————. "Réponse à Aimé Césaire (Introduction à un art poétique haïtien)." *Présence Africaine* 4 (octobre–novembre 1955): 42–62.

Eagleton, Terry. *Marxism and Literary Criticism.* Berkeley and Los Angeles: University of California Press, 1976.

Erickson, John. "Sartre's African Writings: Literature and Revolution." *L'Esprit Créateur* 10 (Fall 1970): 182–96.

Fanon, Frantz. *Les Damnés de la terre.* 2d ed. Paris: François Maspero, 1968.

————. *Peau noire, masques blancs.* 2d ed. Paris: Editions du Seuil/Points, 1975.

Freud, Sigmund. *The Standard Edition of the Complete Psychological Works of Sigmund Freud.* Edited by James Strachey. 24 vols. London: Hogarth Press, 1964.

Frutkin, Susan. *Aimé Césaire: Black between Worlds.* Washington and University of Miami: Center for Advanced International Studies, 1973.

Gauthier, Xavière. *Surréalisme et sexualité.* Préface de J.-B. Pontalis. Paris: Gallimard/Idées, 1971.

Glissant, Edouard. *Le Discours Antillais.* Paris: Seuil, 1981.

————. *L'Intention poétique.* Paris: Seuil, 1969.

Gratiant, Gilbert. "D'une poésie martiniquaise dite nationale." *Présence Africaine* 5 (décembre 1955–janvier 1956): 84–89.

Guérin, Daniel. *Les Antilles décolonisées.* Préface d'Aimé Césaire. Paris: Présence Africaine, 1956.

Hale, Thomas. "Structural Dynamics in a Third World Classic: Aimé Césaire's *Cahier d'un retour au pays natal.*" *Yale French Studies* 53 (1976): 163–74.

————. "Sur *Une tempête* d'Aimé Césaire." *Etudes littéraires* 6 (avril 1973): 21–34.

————, ed. *Les Écrits d'Aimé Césaire: Bibliographie commentée.* Numéro spécial d'*Etudes françaises.* Montreal: Les Presses de l'Université de Montréal, 1978.

Harris, Rodney E. *L'Humanisme dans le théâtre d'Aimé Césaire.* Préface de Thomas Cassirer. Ottawa: Editions Naaman, 1973.

Hegel, G. W. F. *The Phenomenology of Mind.* Translated, with an introduction by J. B. Baillie. Introduction to the Torchbook Edition by George Lichtheim. New York: Harper & Row, 1967.

Jahn, Janheinz. *Muntu, the New African Culture.* Translated by Marjorie Grene. Dusseldorf: Eugene Diederichs Verlag, 1958; New York: Grove Press, 1961.

Jakobson, Roman. *Essais de linguistique générale.* Traduit et préface par Nicolas Ruwet. Paris: Editions de Minuit, 1963.

Jameson, Frederic. "Imaginary and Symbolic in Lacan: Marxism, Psychoanalytic Criticism, and the Problem of the Subject." *Yale French Studies* 55/56 (1977): 338–95.

————. *Marxism and Form.* Princeton: Princeton University Press, 1971.

Jobin, Bruno. "*Cadastre,* lecture transcendante." *Etudes littéraires* 6 (avril 1973): 73–80.

Juin, Hubert. "Aimé Césaire, poète de la liberté." *Présence Africaine* 4 (1948): 564–75.

————. *Aimé Césaire, poète noir.* Paris: Présence Africaine, 1956.

Kesteloot, Lilyan. *Aimé Césaire.* Paris: Seghers, 1962.

————. *Les Ecrivans noirs de langue française: naissance d'une littérature.* 3ème éd. Brussels: Institut de Sociologie de l'Université Libre de Bruxelles, 1965.

Kesteloot, Lilyan, et Kotchy, Barthélemy. *Aimé Césaire, l'homme et l'œuvre.* Précédé d'un texte de Michel Leiris. Paris: Présence Africaine, 1973.

Kristeva, Julia. "Poésie et négativité." *L'Homme* (avril–juin 1968): 36–63.

————. *La Révolution du langage poétique.* Paris: Seuil, 1974.

Lacan, Jacques. *Ecrits.* Paris: Seuil, 1966.

————. *Ecrits I.* Paris: Seuil/Points, 1966.

————. *The Language of the Self. The Function of Language in Psychoanalysis.* Translated with notes and commentary by Anthony Wilden. Baltimore: The Johns Hopkins University Press, 1968; Delta Books, 1968.

Leiner, Jacqueline. "Césaire et les problèmes du langage chez un écrivain francophone." *L'Esprit Créateur* 17, no. 2 (Summer 1977): 133–42.

————. "Entretien avec Aimé Césaire." In *Tropiques,* pp. v–xxiv, ed. Aimé Césaire and René Ménil. Reprint ed. of the complete collection, 2 vols. Paris: Jean-Michel Place, 1978.

————, ed. *Le Soleil éclaté.* Tubingen: Gunter Naar Verlag, 1984.

Leiris, Michel. *Contacts de civilisations en Martinique et en Guadeloupe.* Paris: UNESCO/Gallimard, 1955.

————. "Qui est Aimé Césaire?" Introductory text to *Aimé Césaire, l'homme et l'œuvre,* by Lilyan Kesteloot and Barthélemy Kotchy. Paris: Présence Africaine, 1973. First published in *Critique* 216 (mai 1965).

Les Écrits d'Aimé Césaire. See Thomas Hale.

Lowe, Catherine. "Vers une lecture de 'Totem' d'Aimé Césaire." Paper, Yale University, 1971.

Marcuse, Herbert. *Eros and Civilization.* Boston: Beacon Press, 1955; New York, Vintage Books, 1962.

————. *An Essay on Liberation.* Boston: Beacon Press, 1969.

Mauron, Charles. *Des Metaphores obsédantes au mythe personnel.* Paris: José Corti, 1964.

Mbom, Clément. *Le Théâtre d'Aimé Césaire; ou La Primauté de l'universalité humaine.* Paris: F. Nathan, 1979.

Memmi, Albert. *Portrait du colonisé, précédé du Portrait du colonisateur.* Préface de Jean-Paul Sartre. Paris: Corrêa, 1957; Paris: Pauvert, 1966; Paris: Petite Bibliothèque Payot, 1973.

Meschonnic, Henri. *Pour la poétique III.* Paris: Gallimard, 1973.

Ngal, Georges. "Le Théâtre d'Aimé Césaire: Une dramaturgie de la décolonisation." *Revue des sciences humaines,* 25 (octobre–décembre 1970): 613–36.

Ngal, Mbwil a Mpaang. *Aimé Césaire, un homme à la recherche d'une patrie.* Dakar: Nouvelles Editions Africaines, 1975/83.

Ngaté, Jonathan. " 'Mauvais sang' de Rimbaud et *Cahier d'un retour au pays natal* de Césaire: la poésie au service de la révolution." *Cahiers Césairiens* 3 (printemps 1977): 25–32.

Nietzsche, Friedrich. *The Birth of Tragedy* and *The Genealogy of Morals.* Translated by Francis Golffing. New York: Doubleday Anchor Books, 1956.

———. *The Use and Abuse of History.* Translated by Adrian Collins. Introduction by Julius Kraft. 2d ed. New York: Bobbs-Merrill Co., The Library of Liberal Arts, 1957.

Okam, Hilary. "Aspects of Imagery and Symbolism in the Poetry of Aimé Césaire." *Yale French Studies* 53 (1976): 175–96.

Patri, Aimé. "Deux poètes noirs en langue française: A. Césaire et L. S. Senghor." *Présence Africaine* 3 (1ᵉʳ trimestre 1948): 378–87.

Pigeon, Gérard Georges. "Le Rôle des termes médicaux, du bestiaire et de la flore dans l'imagerie césairienne." *Cahiers Césairiens* 3 (printemps 1977): 7–24.

Riffaterre, Michael. "La métaphore fileé dans la poésie surréaliste." *Langue Française* 3 (septembre 1969): 46–60.

———. *Semiotics of Poetry.* Bloomington and London: Indiana University Press, 1978.

Rimbaud, Arthur. *Oeuvres.* Edition de Suzanne Bernard. Paris: Garnier Frères, 1960.

Santí, Enrico Mario. "The Politics of Poetics." *Diacritics* 8 (Winter 1978): 28–40.

Sartre, Jean-Paul. *L'Être et le néant.* Paris: Gallimard/NRF, 1943.

———. "Orphée noir." Introduction to *Anthologie de la nouvelle poésie nègre et malgache de langue française,* ed. Léopold Sédar Senghor. 2d ed., pp. ix–xliv. Paris: Presses Universitaires de France, 1969.

Scharfman, Ronnie. " 'Corps perdu'—Moi-nègre retrouvé." In *Le Soleil éclaté,* ed. Jacqueline Leiner. Tubingen: Gunter Naar Verlag, 1984.

———. "Repetition and Absence: The Discourse of Deracination in Aimé Césaire's 'Nocturne d'une nostalgie.' " *The French Review* 56 (March 1983): 572–78.

Sellin, Eric. "*Négritude:* Status or Dynamics?" *L'Esprit Créateur* 10 (Fall 1970): 163–81.

Senghor, Léopold Sédar, ed. *Anthologie de la nouvelle poésie nègre et malgache de langue française,* précédée de "Orphée noir" par Jean-Paul Sartre. 2d ed. Paris: Presses Universitaires de France, 1969.

———. *Ethiopiques.* Paris: Seuil, 1956.

———. *Liberté I: négritude et humanisme.* Paris: Seuil, 1964.

———. "Qu'est-ce que la Négritude?" *Etudes françaises* 3 (février 1967): 3–20.

Sieger, Jacqueline. "Entretien avec Aimé Césaire." *Afrique* 5 (octobre 1961): 64–67.

Simmons, Ruth Jean. "The Poetic Language of Aimé Césaire." Ph.D. dissertation, Harvard University, 1973.

Snyder, Emile. "Aimé Césaire: The Reclaiming of the Land." In *Exile and Tradition: Studies in African and Caribbean Literature,* ed. Rowland Smith, pp. 31–43. New York: Africana Publishing Company, 1976.

———. "The Problem of *Négritude* in Modern French Poetry." *Comparative Literature Studies* (1963): 101–14.

―――. "A Reading of Aimé Césaire's *Return to My Native Land.*" *L'Esprit Créateur* 10 (Fall 1970): 197–212.

Songolo, Aliko. "*Cadastre* et *Ferrements* de Césaire. Une nouvelle poétique pour une nouvelle politique." *L'Esprit Créateur* 17, no. 2 (Summer 1977): 143–58.

Stendhal. *De l'Amour.* Chronologie et préface par Michel Crouzel. Paris: Garnier Flammarion, 1965.

Terence. *L'Héautontimorouménos.* Quoted in *Petit Larousse,* 1966 ed. S.v. "Locutions latines et étrangères."

Thomas, Dylan. *Collected Poems.* New York: New Directions, 1957.

Trouillot, Henock. *L'Itinéraire d'Aimé Césaire.* Port-au-Prince, Haiti, 1968.

Walker, Keith Louis. *La Cohésion poétique de l'œuvre césairienne.* Tübingen: Gunter Naar Verlag; Paris: Jean-Michel Place, 1979.

Zadi Zaourou, Bernard. *Césaire entre deux cultures. Problèmes théoriques de la littérature négro-africaine d'aujourd'hui.* Dakar: Les Nouvelles Editions Africaines, 1978.

Index

Africa, 4, 17, 24, 27, 30, 31; culture of, 9, 13, 21, 77; and alienation, 43–44, 46–47
Algeria, 8, 17, 22
Alienation, 102; of blacks, 9, 18, 90; and language, 10, 12–13, 14, 26–27, 31, 99; and colonialism, 11, 12, 25; and the subject, 24, 26, 31, 38, 54, 65; and identity, 29, 43–44, 45, 50, 55, 67, 109–10, 112, 113, 114; geographical model of, 31; and Africa, 43–44
Althusser, Louis, 24
Antilles, the, 4, 9, 13, 14, 18, 23, 26, 31, 39, 40
Apollinaire, Guillaume, 62
Armes miraculeuses, Les, (Césaire), 112; "Le Cristal automatique," 66–69
Arnold, A. James, *Modernism and Negritude: The Poetry and Poetics of Aimé Césaire,* 1, 2, 4, 58n.11, 62n.12

Bachelard, Gaston, 2
Bantu, belief in poetry of, 72
Baudelaire, Charles, 62; "L'Héautontimorouménos," 81
Beckett, Samuel, 71, 102
Benjamin, Walter, 15, 88; "The Author as Producer," 88
Benveniste, Emile, *Problèmes de linguistique générale,* 65, 69, 70, 71, 72, 83
Brecht, Bertolt, 88
Breton, André, 1, 3, 62, 114; *Second Manifeste de Surréalisme,* 78, 107

Cadastre (Césaire), 80, 112; "Mot," 21, 27, 82, 85–92; "Totem," 69–71; "Corps perdu," 74–85, 95; "Barbare," 84
Cahier d'un retour au pays natal (Césaire), 20, 22, 29–64, 101, 112; "discovery" of, 1; discussions of, 4; and Sartre, 6; and

Tel Quel group, 28
Terence, 54
Theater, 3–4, 17. *See also* Césaire,
  Aimé: plays of
Third World, 1, 25
Thomas, Dylan, "Before I knocked,"
  51
Thorez, Maurice, 8
Tropiques, 14

Unconscious, collective, 18

Violence, 20. *See also* Colonialism:
  conflict in

Walker, Keith, *La Cohésion poétique de l'œuvre césairienne,*
  2–3, 74
Woman: as "tu," 47, 58–59,
  65–73, 82; and fertility, 57; and
  sexuality, 57, 72–73

UNIVERSITY OF FLORIDA MONOGRAPHS
HUMANITIES